Here's what others

Your Flight t

G000299985

"Everyone wants to be happy. In this book, Toni Mackenzie will guide you on a journey of 7 powerful steps towards creating the happiness you desire by changing your thoughts, realising you always have choices and learning how to manifest your dreams. I recommend you read it!"

Mike Dooley
New York Times best-selling author of *'Infinite Possibilities'* and contributor to *'The Secret'* DVD and book

"This is a fabulous self-help book. It is easy to read, very engaging from the beginning and has some excellent therapeutic techniques to help readers connect with feelings of happiness. Like all good therapists, Toni has been through some very challenging life experiences but has come through them with knowledge, wisdom and a genuine ability to help others. This book is inspirational, heart-felt and gives readers many keys to finding lasting happiness. Highly recommended!"

Glenn Harrold
Best Selling Author and Hypnotherapist

"A very enlightening book that will help the reader to make sense of their own life and also help them take flight in any direction they wish in their lives."

David R. Hamilton PhD
Best Selling Author of seven books published by Hay House

"Toni Mackenzie's Your Flight to Happiness is about emotional freedom. She shares an inspiring story of her powerful journey and teaches you how to benefit from her discoveries. Her guidance will prove valuable wherever you are on your journey. No-one but you can have your experiences. And no-one but you can change your experiences. Living those principles is the secret of emotional freedom. While they may be hidden in plain sight, a guide like Toni reminds us they're there."

Greg Kuhn
Best selling author of five highly acclaimed books in his *'Why Quantum Physicists...'* series

Your Flight to Happiness
A 7-Step Journey to Emotional Freedom

Copyright @ 2016 Toni Mackenzie

www.innerdepths.co.uk

Toni Mackenzie asserts the moral right to be identified as the author of this book, in accordance with the Copyright, Designs and Patents Act 1988.

First published in 2016 by Inner Depths.

Copyeditor and proof reader: Siân-Elin Flint-Freel

Design and typesetting: Tanya Back

Illustrations: Sladjana Milojevic

Printed and bound: Ingram Spark

ISBN 978-0-9935653-0-4

Your Flight to Happiness

A 7-Step Journey to Emotional Freedom

Toni Mackenzie

I dedicate this book to...

My parents, Margaret and Tony Skellon, for bringing me into this world. With much love and thanks to Mum, who was there to support me at the time of my plane crash and is still always a great support and listening ear when I need one, and in loving memory of Dad, whose past gentleness, love and support is greatly appreciated and sadly missed.

My precious children, Marcus and Melissa Mackenzie. Thank you both for coming into my life and enabling me to fulfil one of my biggest dreams by becoming your mum. I love you both very much.

In loving memory of my grandparents, Mary and Eddie Ward — my wonderful Nan played a huge part in my upbringing and my lovely Granddad was always there in the background with his little jokes and dry sense of humour.

Contents

Happiness is an Inside Job.

Pre-flight Information

Everyone wants to be happy, but so many people believe that happiness is something they can only possibly have at sometime in the future, once they have the right circumstances, partner, possessions or money they desire. The problem is, the future never comes, so we go through life wanting and not getting, wanting and getting, getting and losing, and continue searching for happiness in the wrong places. The reality is happiness has been inside us all along, just waiting to be discovered and released.

Some of your life experiences and material possessions can, of course, *help* you to feel happy — for a while. You can feel good while pampering yourself, eating delicious food, enjoying the company of people you like or love, wearing a new outfit that makes you feel good or having fabulous holidays but the happiness you feel as a result of anything outside of you either comes to an end or it can be taken away from you.

True, lasting happiness cannot be taken away from you; it comes from changing the way you think. Most of the thoughts that prevent you from feeling happy now are avoidable and within your control. They are all too often about trivial, petty things, things we cannot change, things that happened in the past, things that just may possibly happen in the future — things that really don't need to affect how you feel in the present. Your thoughts, whether positive or negative, create your beliefs, your expectations and your attitude and, together, they affect the way that you feel, emotionally and physically.

I meet people, know people and read about people every day who are not happy but who could be if they only knew how to free themselves from their self-imposed emotional pain. I've written this book because I want to help people realise that they have the power to change their lives by changing their thoughts.

I know from personal experience that the lessons I share in this book are both powerful and practical. I've used them along my own journey and, as a result, have moved from feeling a profound sense of inner sadness, emptiness and incompleteness to feeling happiness, contentment and inner strength — most of the time. Of course we are all human and it's likely that you will feel upset, annoyed or anxious about things in your life from time to time but by using these tools you'll find that it will happen less and less. When it does happen, you'll become aware of any unhelpful feelings much more quickly, see them for what they are and be able to let them go.

My own journey has been something of a long-haul, multi-stop flight and, along the way, I've changed my life totally in so many positive ways. I've read, studied and learned from the wisdom shared by some of the most enlightened philosophers, teachers and writers from the East and the West and I continue to learn and grow more with every single day. To help you reach your destination more quickly than I did, I've condensed the main lessons I've learned so far into just seven steps that you can take on your short-haul flight to freedom and happiness.

If you want to find true, lasting happiness, you need to learn how to F.L.Y. ~ First Love Yourself

Throughout the chapters, when you see the wings image, it will be followed by a 'Flying Lesson' which will help you to grow your wings and learn to F.L.Y. — First Love Yourself — an essential ingredient of happiness.

I strongly recommend that you use a special journal or notebook to record your thoughts, feelings, challenges and 'Aha!' moments while working through your flying lessons. You can divide it into sections and also use it to write down your goals and intentions, as well as any inspirational quotes or ideas that you want to remember. You can also make notes on the blank 'Thoughts' pages at the end of each chapter.

Before you begin your journey, I'd like to share with you a little more about how I got from where I was to where I am now...

The shell must break
before the bird can fly.

~ Alfred Lord Tennyson

The Plane Crash

My world is turned upside down...

One day while I was working as an air stewardess, a passenger I'd seen a few times on previous flights wrote me a note. He told me he was was an airline pilot who was based overseas but travelled home to the UK regularly and asked if he could take me out for dinner. One of the other stewardesses who knew him passed the note to me so I asked her about him. She gave him a good reference and I agreed to go out with him the next time he was home. Over the following months, he wined and dined me in all the top restaurants whenever he was home in the UK, but there was nothing serious between us as he was out of the country much of the time.

A few weeks later, a passenger I'd seen once before on a previous flight wrote me a note. I recognised him as a well-known TV and film actor and it had been all over the press that he'd been asked to audition for the role of James Bond. His note read simply, *Are we a mile high yet?* He was referring to the 'Mile High Club' which, for anyone who hasn't heard of it, is a term applied to anyone who's had sex in an aircraft while at least a mile above ground level. This very cheeky note was written on his napkin so that I couldn't help but see it when I collected his coffee tray. As a rather prim and proper former convent school girl, I was really shocked! Although I was confident in my role as an air stewardess in general, I didn't feel at all confident about how to handle this situation. I felt embarrassed, so I just ignored his note and avoided catching his eye for the rest of the flight!

When we arrived at our destination, he stayed in his seat until all the other passengers had disembarked and then he walked down to the exit looking very awkward. He apologised profusely saying that his note was a stupid joke and he really hadn't meant to offend me. He seemed as embarrassed about having written it as I'd been when I read it and I could tell that his apology was sincere. He told me he lived in London but visited his family in Merseyside regularly and asked if he could take me out to dinner the next time he was in town. I told him I'd have to think about it but agreed to give him my phone number. He had to call me several times from London before I finally agreed to go on a date with him.

During one of our phone conversations I mentioned that I also did some photographic modelling work for catalogues and TV adverts. He asked me to post him a copy of my modelling photo card and, after recieving it, he sent me a lovely hand-written letter saying how much he loved my pictures and that he was carrying my card around with him. (This was all done by post in the days before emails and smartphones!) He eventually won me over with his charm and humour and we arranged our first dinner date.

As a result, for a short period of time I was dating both the pilot and the actor, but there was no pressure on me to decide between the two, so I decided to take things one day at a time and see how it all progressed. The pilot had already told me he'd be home for Christmas and would like to be with me as much as possible during that time. I then heard from the actor who told me he was going to be staying at his parents' home over the Christmas period and wanted me to join him there to meet the family. It was decision time...

After giving the situation much consideration, I decided that because I'd known the pilot longer, had agreed to see him over Christmas sooner, and the actor could well be disappearing off to Hollywood in the near future, I'd stick with the pilot. This decision meant I had to bring my dalliance with the actor to an end.

Over Christmas, the pilot told me he wanted us to be in a committed relationship. I agreed and, over the following months, we fell in love and decided to get married. I'd been promoted to a position of Line-Training Stewardess, responsible for in-flight training and interviewing new recruits as well as normal flying duties. I enjoyed my job but, as he was working overseas and we wanted to spend as much time as possible together, I was happy to give up my career so I was free to travel with him.

Once we were married, we both wanted to start a family as soon as possible so he decided to come back and work for a UK-based airline. A few house moves ensued over the following years while he was initially based at different airports, including Birmingham, Cardiff and Glasgow. We were both delighted when he was eventually able to move back to the Manchester area where we wanted to put down our roots.

While moving around the UK we'd lived in several rented houses and knew exactly what features we wanted and what we didn't want in a house, so my husband decided that he was going to build our ideal home. After searching for a while we found a wonderful plot of land in Cheshire and together we designed our dream six-bedroom house.

Although we'd wanted children from the start, it didn't happen easily; however, after a few years of various tests, treatments and prayers, we were eventually blessed with a gorgeous baby boy, followed almost three years later by a beautiful baby girl. By the time we started building the house, our son was six and our daughter was three and I loved being a full-time mum. I felt loved by my husband and was very excited that we'd soon be moving into our wonderful new home. I had everything I wanted in my life and felt very contented.

Over the years we were together, I joined my husband on several trips overseas to the Far East, the Middle East, the USA and Africa, as well as various destinations in Europe. He was always very affectionate, demonstrative and complimentary, and wanted to be with me as much as possible. He even frequently swapped his long-haul flights with other pilots so he could stay at home with me.

The last time I joined him was while he was on a training course in Miami. He asked me to fly out with our son so we could take him to Disneyworld in Orlando, and we all had a wonderful week together. However, soon after I returned home, I discovered something that sent the plane in which I was happily cruising along come crashing down to the ground...

My husband had been having an affair with a married woman. At first I was in a state of total shock and disbelief. After finding photographs of them in compromising positions in a hotel room together and explicit letters she had written to him, the truth sank in and I felt physically sick to my stomach. I felt so betrayed and hurt and I knew that things could never be the same between us again, no matter what happened from that moment on.

I told him I wanted a divorce and at first he tried to talk me out of it but there was no way I could accept what he'd done and stay married to him. When he realised I was determined to go ahead, he persuaded me to wait until the house was finished. He told me we couldn't sell a half-built house and to sell it when completed without living in it would have involved paying a large amount of capital gains tax. He said we should move into it but we could sleep in separate bedrooms, live separate lives, then sell it after a year and divide the equity.

Despite my reluctance, I agreed to this after he convinced me that it would be the best thing for the children and that if I didn't agree there would be little or no equity left to split. I didn't feel I had much choice but to go along with his decision. He was in control of our finances and despite what he'd done I trusted that he was doing what was best for us financially.

Although I won't go into everything that happened from that

time until the house was sold because it's not relevant to this book, I will tell you it was the most horrendous period of my life. I wasn't strong or assertive back then and he took advantage of my vulnerability. I'd never before felt so completely powerless and out of control of what was happening to me. Because I didn't have any personal income, I had to ask him for money every time I needed to buy groceries and petrol, giving him receipts for everything I spent. He seemed to love the feeling of power he had over me and would openly laugh about it.

When I came across a box of cassette tapes and some trailing wires in a spare bedroom cupboard, I realised that the home phone was being tapped (I didn't have a mobile phone) and he'd been listening to all of my private phone conversations. I felt absolutely violated and sickened that he'd even taken away my privacy. Much as I wanted to be free of him, I felt that I couldn't just move out; I had no income and nowhere to go to and I wanted to protect the children from any unecessary hardship.

He later told me I had to sign a legal document stating how the equity would be split after any debts were paid off. I was a little suspicious but when I held back he made threats about making life even more difficult for me. I eventually signed as I knew that there were no debts apart from the mortgage. Little did I know that in doing this I'd given him carte blanche to create as many 'debts' as he liked over the following year. This enabled him to appear with a document on moving day stating that every penny of the equity was going to be used to pay off these so-called debts. Almost unbelieveably, one debt that he'd listed was for a light aircraft he'd supposedly bought from his mistress...but because I'd signed that document I couldn't legally do anything about it.

Once again, I felt like I'd been kicked in the stomach. He'd managed to trick me out of my share of the equity and I had nothing. In anticipation of receiving my money, I'd found a house to rent for six months, intending to find somewhere to buy within that time, and was due to move in that day. Now, I was in no position to do this so I called my solicitor, who advised me to stay put and refuse to move out. When I told my ex of his advice, his response was to laugh and turn off the power supply so there was no heat or light, attempting to force me out with the children.

We should have moved out hours earlier but, because of the problems and delays, it was late afternoon on a winter's day and beginning to turn dark. The removal van was waiting outside filled with our belongings and the footballer and his wife who'd bought our house were outside waiting to move in. I was in a desperate situation and had no choice but to stand my ground until eventually he very reluctantly and angrily agreed to pay the rental agency six months' rent in advance just to get us out.

The next day he called my son's school and my daughter's nursery school, telling them they wouldn't be going back. He then dropped a note through my new front door informing me that he was no longer going to pay the children's school fees — and it was my fault for forcing him to pay the rent!

The whole experience left me devastated and I could not believe the deceitful way he'd behaved, but I still felt that as a well-paid airline pilot he would at least be made to pay child support. I had no idea that things were about to get even worse when, very soon after, he quit his job and told the court he was unemployed. Soon after the court case was closed, he took a new job with an airline overseas and, because he was working out of the country, the Child Support Agency were powerless to make him pay anything.

He didn't say goodbye to the children and never attempted to contact them again. They were both understandably very confused and our six-year-old son was particularly hurt as he'd had a very close relationship with his father. He kept asking me where Daddy had gone and when he was coming back.

So there I was, a single mother with two very young children, jobless, penniless and facing a future of being homeless in six months' time. I could have given up completely and gone to pieces and, if anyone had asked me beforehand what I'd do if I were ever to be in such a situation, that's exactly what I would have predicted.

What actually happened was that this experience in my life, which felt devastating at the time, eventually led me to discover the inner strength I didn't know I had. It steered me to embark upon a path of self-development, self-growth and, ultimately, self-empowerment and I'll be telling you how I achieved this in the following chapters.

When everything seems
to be going against you, remember
that the airplane takes off against
the wind, not with it.
~ Henry Ford

Before we move forward, let me briefly take you back to a much earlier time, to the time where life began for me...

Margaret and Tony met at the iconic Rialto Ballroom in Liverpool, dancing to the sounds of the resident 12-piece orchestra. As well as being a snappy dresser, 22-year-old Tony was a pretty good jiver who had won several competitions. He was in the Merchant Navy, working in the cocktail bar on cruise ships which sailed to and from the USA (where he bought his stylish suits and shoes). Margaret was a pretty 19-year-old who worked as a waitress in an exclusive private member's dining club in Liverpool's affluent Abercromby Square area and loved to go dancing in the evenings. They fell in love, got married and, fifteen months later, their first baby was born, a daughter who they named Antonia, otherwise known as Toni — me!

Mum gave up work to become a full-time mother, bringing up my two younger brothers and I, with five years between each of us. She loved buying me beautiful clothes, dressing me up and taking me out, and soon became a self-taught expert dressmaker who was able to copy any of the expensive dresses she would see in the stores.

Although Dad was frequently away on trips across the Atlantic, it was always very exciting when he came home on leave, especially when he opened his suitcase and brought out all kinds of wonderful presents. I have treasured memories of him taking me to 'The Tatler' (a quaint little cinema in Liverpool town centre) to watch Walt Disney films and then to the 'Majorca Café' where we'd have chocolate or strawberry ice cream.

Mum was raised as a Roman Catholic, as was her mother and many generations of her family before her but Dad didn't follow any particular religion. He was a gentle, easy-going soul who'd grown up in the countryside with his precious pet ferret, he loved jazz music and always had a book on the go, and he was happy for me to be raised in the same religion as mum and her family.

So that's where I came from... In the next chapter, you'll read about how everyone's early childhood experiences impact their development into adulthood and, throughout this book, I'll be referring back to some of my later childhood experiences and how they influenced the choices and decisions I made at various stages of my life. These examples will help to illustrate how I became who I *thought* I was at the time of my crash landing and how, by changing my thinking, I was able to heal my broken wings and learn to fly again, eventually flying higher than ever before...

Be as a bird perched on a frail branch that she feels bending beneath her, still she sings away all the same, knowing she has wings.
~ Victor Hugo

Thoughts

There is freedom waiting for you, on the breezes of the sky, and you ask 'What if I fall?' Oh but my darling, what if you fly?

~ Erin Hanson

Step 1

Fear of Flying...
or Fear of Failing?

Limiting Beliefs

Do you have a fear of flying or is it a fear of failing? Would you like to reach for the sky but are too afraid you'll fall? Maybe you're afraid to step out of your comfort zone...or could it be that your 'comfort zone' is actually your discomfort zone?

Just pause for a moment and think about where you are right now and where you'd really like to be. Ask yourself, *What's been holding me down so far?* It's impossible to fly when you're carrying a heavy weight. If you've wanted to fly for years but still not managed to take that first leap of faith, read on...

"It's impossible to fly when you're carrying a heavy weight."

You were born with only two fears: the fear of falling and the fear of loud noises. Any other fears, including worries, anxieties or phobias, have been created by your life experiences. You may be afraid of failing or you may be afraid of succeeding. You may have a fear of being ridiculed, being alone, being rejected, being hurt or being poor, and these fears may be holding you back and stopping you from being happy.

Fear can, of course, be realistic and protect us from putting ourselves in genuinely dangerous situations, but all too often irrational fears are created by the power of our imagination. When we spend time imagining the things that might go wrong, we create the same uncomfortable feelings within ourselves as if they already have. Worrying about the possibility of negative outcomes can also cause us to hold back in life and miss out on new opportunities and experiences, limiting the quality of our lives.

There are two primary emotions: one is fear and the other is love. All negative emotions stem from fear, including anger, depression, stress, anxiety, hatred, guilt, resentment and blame. All positive emotions come from love, including kindness, peace, gratitude, awe, contentment, joy and happiness. Step 1 of your flight to Happiness involves becoming aware of what it is you're afraid of and where those fears have come from so you can start to let them go and move towards a state of love, which is essential for happiness.

So many people go through life without ever being aware that their deep-rooted fears are stopping them from achieving their goals, blocking them from manifesting their dreams, and preventing them from reaching their full potential. Consciously, we may think that we want to achieve certain goals, but the limiting beliefs we've developed as a result of our fears are stopping us from doing so. These beliefs are held in our subconscious minds and lead to the thoughts that we think, over and over again. As we think around 65,000 thoughts each day, you can probably get an idea of just how powerful your mind is in creating how you feel, act and react!

As Henry Ford, founder of the Ford Motor Company, famously said, *If you think you can do a thing or you think you can't, you're right.* In other words, if you tell yourself something often enough, it becomes a belief

"If you think you can do a thing or you think you can't, you're right."

and consequently it will become a reality, a 'self-fulfilling prophecy'. So, you can see why it makes sense to become aware of your thoughts and words, and choose to make them positive ones.

Your mind is divided into two parts, only 5-10% is conscious and in your awareness, the other 90-95% is subconscious, or unconscious, and hidden beneath the surface. The conscious mind is the part you use when you are focusing, planning, and paying full attention to something. Without having to think about it, your powerful subconscious mind keeps your heart beating and your lungs breathing, controls your digestive system and your nervous system, and keeps all of your bodily functions working without any conscious effort from you.

When you first learned to crawl, walk, ride a bike, drive a car or any other skill that was new to you, you needed to give your full conscious attention to the task in hand but, once learned through repetition, you were able to do these things without even thinking. If you drive, how many times have you driven somewhere and not remembered the journey? When your conscious mind is diverted and wanders off elsewhere, the subconscious part of your mind takes over and drives the car for you as if it's on autopilot.

Your subconscious mind is continuously taking in information as well as storing every memory of every experience you've ever had. It can be likened to a seven-year-old child as, during the first six or seven years of your life, it downloaded information from the messages you received from your parents or carers. Those messages include the words that were spoken to you, those spoken about you and those which were unspoken but clearly implied by the actions and reactions of the influential adults around you.

Of those 65,000 thoughts you have each day, the chances are that around 90% of them are negative. Are you allowing a harsh critic to live inside your head, telling you you're likely to fail, you're not worthy of love, you'll never be happy,

"Are you allowing a harsh critic to live inside your head?"

other people are better in some way than you, you can't do it (whatever 'it' may be) and so on?

If someone is being abusive, continuously insulting you and putting you down, it doesn't make it easy for you to feel happy, does it? To make things worse, when you feel bad about yourself, other people pick up your unspoken signals of self-doubt or low self-esteem and are likely to treat you accordingly, reinforcing your beliefs and causing the negative cycle to continue.

You may well have downloaded the limiting belief that you shouldn't be proud of yourself or 'blow your own trumpet' because you'll appear conceited. You may find it much easier to play down or even reject compliments from others rather than accepting them gracefully. You may generally tend to focus on what you believe is wrong with you, rather than what's right... Well now it's time for you to become fully aware of just what your inner critic is telling you, stop allowing it to put you down and start being kinder to yourself, the way you are towards people you love and care about. It's time to learn how to love and care for yourself!

When my marriage suddenly ended, one of my first thoughts — which immediately led to feelings of fear and panic — was that I no longer had someone who loved me.

"Loving yourself is not about arrogance; it's about self-acceptance."

Of course I knew my children loved me, but I believed that I *needed* a partner to love me in order to really feel lovable. Over the years that followed, as I learned to take responsibility for my life, I also learned to take responsibility for loving myself.

Loving yourself is not about arrogance; it's about self-acceptance. It's accepting yourself unconditionally as the unique human being you are and loving yourself, 'warts and all'...

Flying Lesson 1:
The Negative Thought Stopping Exercise

Before you can change the negative, critical thoughts going around in your head that are causing you to feel unworthy, fearful and unhappy, you need to become aware of just what you're saying to yourself.

A very effective way of doing this is to place a rubber band around your wrist and, whenever it catches your eye, pause and check what your inner voice is saying. If it's criticising, complaining, moaning, worrying, comparing yourself to others, telling yourself off, saying something 'isn't fair' or anything else negative, firmly command it to *STOP*, ping your elastic band and replace the negative thought with a positive one.

At first, as soon as your conscious attention goes back to what you were doing, the chatterbox will come creeping in again because it's not used to being stopped; it's had free rein for years! Don't give up or berate yourself when this happens; it's a bit like training a puppy, if you keep repeating a command, the message will eventually sink in and the desired response will then become automatic.

If you commit to doing this for a week or so, you'll soon find that those old negative thoughts become less and less until they're hardly ever there and, if they do occasionally pop up, you'll notice them straight away and stop them in their tracks!

As you start to notice the negative messages you're repeating to yourself, write them down in your journal or notepad. You could divide a page into two columns, write the negative message on the left side and, on the right side, write down a positive message to replace it. You'll learn more about how to create positive messages, or affirmations, in Step 2.

He who would learn to fly
one day must first learn to stand
and walk and run and climb and dance;
one cannot fly into flying.

~ Friedrich Nietzsche

We were all born with the potential to shine in our own unique way but in so many cases this potential becomes buried, hidden beneath the layers of self-doubt and fear that form around us. Your personality and traits were created by everything you were exposed to throughout your life, some good, some not so good.

Everything you saw, heard and felt, everything that was passed on to you by your parents, extended family, teachers and other influential adults, and every single life experience you've had has, at some stage, been downloaded into your subconscious mind. These early experiences and childhood messages formed your early thoughts and beliefs, which in turn created your perception of who you were, what you were capable of, and how you viewed the world.

For most people there were at least some experiences and messages which were positive, as well as some that were not so positive, and some which were downright negative but, once something has been accepted into your subconscious mind, it becomes part of your belief system and isn't easy to shift. If, for instance, you learned to believe that you weren't very good at certain activities or that you wouldn't ever be able to achieve certain things, then the likelihood is that you won't be able to do or achieve those things, reinforcing your belief and continuing the cycle.

Overall I remember my early years as being happy and carefree. At home I enjoyed painting and colouring-in, playing with my many dolls, riding my bike and having fun with friends on the street where we lived. I was regularly taken out shopping by my mum and nan to stylish clothes shops, department stores and shoe shops.

I must have particularly loved shoe shops as I've been told that our living room was regularly transformed into a shoe shop, with me as the 'shoe shop lady'. Mum and Nan indulged me by coming into my 'shop' and trying on lots of high-heeled shoes before deciding which pair to buy. Those early experiences may well explain why over the years I've had a penchant for buying beautiful shoes and now have a somewhat excessive collection in my walk-in wardrobe!

Nan later bought her own shop and I loved helping out there, often dressing the windows with the ladies' clothes and jewellery she sold, and the idea of one day becoming a window dresser really appealed to me. At that time most shops, including Nan's, were closed on Wednesday afternoons so after school she used to often take me to the cinema, which was in the same Rialto Buildings that housed her shop and also the Rialto Ballroom where Mum and Dad had met.

At the cinema I particularly loved watching Hollywood musicals where glamorous people wined, dined and danced in stylish restaurants and nightclubs, wearing fabulous gowns. At home I'd spend hours flicking through my collection of 'film star books', admiring the beautiful female movie stars with their long hair, red lipstick and gorgeous dresses, and I developed a love of drawing both female faces and women in fashionable outfits.

These were all positive experiences for me and I'm sure that they've continued to influence my preferences and choices throughout life. I still love shopping, fashionable clothes, high heels, make-up, wining and dining in stylish restaurants and a fair bit of glamour — as well as lots of other more serious things in life of course!

Nan was a strong woman and we were very close. Mum, Dad and I lived with her and Grandad for the first few years of my life, which worked well for Mum as Dad was away at sea more often than he was at home. Even when we later moved to our own house further down the same street, Nan often used to stay there with Mum and I while Dad was away.

I remember her telling me at some stage that I didn't have to worry about getting qualifications at school as girls got married, had children and stayed at home to raise them. I accepted what she said as fact, especially as Mum had given up work when pregnant with me and I assumed that I'd follow in her footsteps.

"Young children absorb information without question and it then becomes hard-wired into their subconscious minds, whether or not it's true."

Young children absorb information without question and it then becomes hard-wired into their subconscious minds, whether or not it's true.

Looking back it seems surprising that I didn't question what she'd said when the reality was that she worked hard all her life! She started off as a waitress and later became a restaurant manager, before buying her own retail business in her late forties and running it until she retired. Even then she took a part-time job in a local gift shop, working there until her late seventies, and still had all her wits about her right up until her death at the age of 94.

I have no doubt that she meant well when she said what she did, but the message I downloaded was that a woman's place was in the home. I imagine she just wanted me, like her daughter, to have what she felt would be an easier life than she'd had.

● ●

Most parents, even the most loving, caring ones, have little or no idea just how much they're conditioning their children by passing down the limiting beliefs they're carrying from their own programming. The 'shoulds' and 'shouldn'ts', as well as the fears, beliefs, values, prejudices, expectations and behaviours that have been passed down to you may go back generations. Perhaps no-one in previous generations of your family has ever questioned whether they're right or true, or considered whether or not they should continue to be passed on to their children. Perhaps, unlike you, they didn't ever get to a point where they realised they could change their programming, release their limiting beliefs, and set themselves free.

As well as parental messages, there are all the messages you received from teachers in school, the education system, bullies in the playground, religious dogma and rules, images and stories in the media — what's acceptable and what's unacceptable. You may have learned that you were not clever enough, not talented enough, not slim enough, not pretty or good looking enough, not 'cool' enough, and began to believe that you were inadequate and just 'not good enough'...

The negative messages I received during childhood were mainly through the church. From as far back as I can remember, I was dutifully taken to mass on Sundays and holy days of obligation and, when I was five years old, I started at the local Catholic convent primary school for girls. This was the beginning of the serious business of indoctrination with man-made religious dogma, which included teachings of guilt, shame, lowliness and inadequacy.

I learned that mortal sins, which included missing mass on Sundays or holy days, eating meat on Fridays, using contraception, having sex before marriage, getting a divorce or even entering a non-Catholic church would result in me 'burning in hell' when I died.

From the age of six, I was obliged to go to church every Saturday evening, get down on my knees in a booth, confess my 'sins' to the priest and ask for forgiveness. As it was assumed by the church that I was a 'sinner', to say that I didn't have any sins to confess would have certainly been considered a 'sin' in itself, so I had to try really hard to come up with some 'bad' thoughts or deeds to confess.

Rather than encouraging children to acknowledge the positive things they'd done and help them to develop a healthy sense of self-esteem (this would have been seen as pride — one of the seven deadly sins!), the church's teachings seemed aimed at convincing us that we were unworthy sinners. Not really surprising that my sense of self-worth started to go downhill and I began to develop feelings of not being 'good enough'.

I passed the eleven plus exam and went on to the local Catholic convent grammar school for girls. Apart from art and sculpture classes and the art teacher, who was very encouraging and nurturing, my memories of school are generally very negative. The headmistress was a surly nun who walked around the corridors of the school in her black and white habit, looking for anything she could find to criticise or complain about. I don't recall ever seeing her smile or hearing her utter a positive word. She had the demeanour of an angry jailer, but with rosary beads jangling from her waist instead of keys.

This woman of the church seemed to enjoy getting students up on the raised stage at assembly while she humiliated them in front of the whole school. This demoralising experience was the punishment for such 'crimes' as being seen outside school without your hat (a ridiculously designed skull cap which continuously slipped off your head) or not being able to tell her the colour of the priest's garments at the previous Sunday afternoon Benediction service. She was also well-practised at forcefully slapping palms with the leather slipper she carried around in her pocket while grimacing menacingly at her victims.

The years I spent there were definitely endured rather than enjoyed. It was hardly comparable to Solomon Northup's horrific experiences, recorded in the book 'Twelve Years a Slave', but after twelve years a convent schoolgirl, the caged bird was finally set free. It just took her a while longer to discover that she could fly...

• •

Over the years in my role as a therapist, I've worked with so many people who have been damaged deeply by their early childhood messages. Men and women of all ages and from many different walks of life confide in me about how insecure they feel in their relationships, their jobs, their social lives and their financial situation. I meet people with successful careers who feel like they're impostors and fear they are about to be 'found out' as well as people who worry incessantly about what other people think of them.

There are those with loving partners who don't believe they deserve them so they act in a way that pushes them away. Because of their limiting beliefs that their partner will cheat or leave them, they create self-fulfilling prophecies, then when their prediction comes true, they are able to say, *See, I was right, I knew he would leave me,* and feel strangely self-righteous. Their experiences reinforce their beliefs so they continue to sabotage their chances of having a happy, loving relationship.

I've worked with many clients who have spent their lives 'staying small' for fear of even putting themselves in positions where they might feel vulnerable. They avoid relationships altogether or engage in unhealthy ones and allow their partners to call the shots and control them while they act like doormats. Some stay in dead-end or challenging jobs for years on end because they don't believe they're worthy of even applying for more rewarding, better-paid positions.

So many clients I've seen crave love, admiration or approval from others to help them feel better because they don't love or respect themselves. They feel a false and temporary sense of happiness while a partner is showing them love or friends and colleagues tell them how wonderful they are but, when that partner leaves them, they're dropped by a friend, or do something to lose respect in the workplace, they feel devastated and need to find a new partner, friend or job as their fragile ego has been crushed. None of these people were born feeling the way they do. They've all been negatively programmed and formed limiting beliefs about themselves, their abilities and their self-worth, causing them to feel fearful and unhappy.

So how do I help them to set themselves free from fear and find happiness from the inside? I teach them how to stop operating on autopilot and take back control of their subconscious mind using the seven steps to emotional freedom

"If you want to fly, you have to break free from the chains that have been holding you down."

I'm sharing with you in this book. If you want to fly, you have to break free from the chains that have been holding you down. By following these steps you can begin to let go of the limiting beliefs you've downloaded, change your mindset, learn to love, value, respect and believe in yourself, then reach for the sky and soar towards Happiness! Are you ready to prepare for your journey?

Aerodynamically the bumblebee shouldn't be able to fly, but the bumblebee doesn't know that so it goes on flying anyway.
~ Mary Kay Ash

Flying Lesson 2:
Childhood Messages Exercise

Once something has been accepted into your subconscious mind at a young age, it becomes part of your belief system and it's going to stay there unless you become aware that it's there, question it and, if it isn't working for you, make a conscious effort to change it. The exercise below can help you become aware of the childhood messages you were given (good and bad, spoken or unspoken) and determine if they are still affecting you as an adult. You may have been given the message that you were good at certain things but would never be able to achieve others or even that you didn't deserve them. You may have grown up feeling that your family were more (or less) worthy than other families and perhaps that you should only mix with people from a similar background. You may have downloaded the belief that having lots of money was your birthright or, alternatively, that money was the root of all evil. To help you become more aware of your childhood messages, positive and negative, complete the exercise below.

Consider the messages you received about the five topics below:
1. Self-worth
2. Relationships
3. Love
4. Money
5. Religion

Take out your journal or notepad and first of all write down any messages you received about each one of the topics from your parents or main carers. Next make another list of the messages you received about the same topics from outside your home (school, church, extended family, media etc.), then finally write down your current beliefs about each of the topics.

Reflect on how much your early programming may still be affecting your current beliefs. Any messages that have influenced your choices and behaviour in a positive way you'll obviously want to keep, but if you become aware of any messages that have been holding you back or causing you pain, you have completed the first step towards removing them.

If doing the exercise above has brought up any negative feelings towards your parents, it's important to remember that they were born as innocent babies and became programmed by their parents, just as their parents were before them. You may be a parent yourself and be feeling guilty about how you may have negatively affected your own children, but know that we are all doing the best that we can from our current state of awareness at any given time. When our awareness changes, so do our attitude and our behaviour.

Having now become aware of your childhood messages and limiting beliefs it's time for Step 2 where you will learn how to begin to change any hard-wired beliefs with which you've been programmed.

Thoughts

Thoughts

You were born with greatness. You were born with wings. You are not meant for crawling, so don't. You have wings. Learn to use them and fly.

~ Rumi

Step 2

Switch off the Autopilot

Affirmations and Autosuggestion

It's time to create a new flight plan. Autopilot is a great thing as long as the plane is going in the right direction, but not so good if it's gone off course and you don't like where it's going.

"Autopilot is a great thing as long as the plane is going in the right direction..."

Now that you've realised you've been operating on autopilot all these years, it's time to switch it off, create a new flight plan and change direction so your life can go exactly where you want it to — onwards and upwards...

Just take a few minutes to imagine your conscious mind as the captain and your subconscious thoughts as the passengers on the plane. Use the power of your mind to imagine yourself sitting in the pilot's seat and those passengers behind you in the cabin criticising you, insulting you, and trying to distract you. They're shouting out things like *You'll never be happy, There's no point in trying, It won't work, You can't change, You're useless, You haven't got what it takes, You should just give up.*

But you are the captain and you are in control, not the passengers, and you're no longer prepared to listen to the nonsense they're spouting. You have the power to order that rabble in the back to be quiet or get off your plane, so imagine yourself doing that firmly and with authority and let them know that you are now taking back control. Watch out though, those critics may have been silenced or sent packing for now, but they tend to be very persistent. That's why it's so important to work on your new flight plan which will keep you on track towards your destination of Happiness.

Just as the repetition of negative messages creates deep-rooted beliefs, so can the repetition of positive self-talk, otherwise known as autosuggestion or affirmations.

Autosuggestion is a form of self-hypnosis developed by a French pharmacist named Emile Coué. In his book, 'Self-Mastery through Conscious Auto-suggestion', he taught how to consciously reprogramme the mind by repeating posi-tive phrases such as, *Every day in every way, I am getting better and better.* This phrase is still widely used as the wording is very general and can be used for a variety of issues — physical, mental and emotional.

> **"Every day in every way, I am getting better and better."**

Coué was also one of the first people to acknowledge what is now known as the placebo effect. This occurs when someone is given a treatment with no known effectiveness, believing that it will heal their condition. There have been hundreds of reports of patients recovering from all kinds of illnesses after being given a sugar pill or a saline injection, which they believed were drugs, osteoarthritis sufferers experiencing pain relief after undergoing fake knee operations, and people growing hair after using a bland lotion which they were told was a powerful hair restorer.

The 'no-cebo' effect occurs when people are given a 'dummy' drug or treatment and are told that they are likely to experience side effects such as nausea or drowsiness. The result is that they experience those effects even though the treatment was actually harmless.

There are also many verified stories of people who were diagnosed with a terminal illness and told they had a limited time to live. Their health started to rapidly deteriorate because they believed they were dying, but when they were told that their diagnosis had been incorrect, their symptoms immediately disappeared and they fully recovered. These experiences are proof of the incredible power of the thoughts that you think and the beliefs that you hold in your mind.

Affirmations are phrases which you can use to reprogramme your mind and change the thoughts you think and the beliefs you hold. To undo the damage created by your early conditioning, you need to replace the childhood messages and limiting beliefs you uncovered in Step 1 with new positive messages and beliefs. Instead of telling yourself *I can't*, you begin to tell yourself *I can*. Instead of criticising yourself, you look in the mirror and tell yourself *I love you, you're amazing.*

When you're able to accept that what you're saying isn't yet true, but you decide that you are going to keep repeating it anyway until it is you create an allowance for the affirmations to begin to work. Repeating a couple of affirmations is not going to magically change how you feel overnight but it will begin the process of changing how your mind works. Continuing to use affirmations on a daily basis will, however, very soon start to change your beliefs and how you feel about yourself.

Unfortunately, when I first discovered affirmations as a teenager, I didn't understand this and found that they had the opposite effect to the one I was hoping for. Over recent years I've discovered a way of creating much more powerful and effective affirmations and I'll be sharing this with you later in the chapter.

• •

As I mentioned in the first chapter, from a young age I was taken out shopping to smart shops and department stores regularly. I have memories of often being told that I had to be a 'good girl' and if I did anything that wasn't considered good girl behaviour, I'd receive a tug on my arm and be told, *Everyone is looking at you.*

I'm sure that it was well-meant and said with the intention of teaching me to behave in a certain way in public and, as an adult, I know it wouldn't have been true that everyone, if indeed anyone, was looking. However, at that very young age, those words made feel embarrassed and very conscious of what other people might be thinking of me. The fact that I can remember this happening so many years later proves to me just how much those early experiences affected me.

My concerns about what other people might think of me stayed and became stronger until, at some stage when I was older, I remember hearing it said, both to me and about me, that I was 'very self-conscious'. I then felt that this was a fault in me, which further knocked my self-esteem. I obviously wasn't born self-conscious but as a result of those early experiences I learned to believe that other people were likely to be judging me.

There were many other messages and experiences, especially throughout my early teen years, which knocked my confidence and self-esteem and caused me to feel unhappy. These combined with the religious messages of unworthiness I'd downloaded and my negative convent school experiences; it's not surprising that I didn't grow up to be a confident teenager.

I hated feeling so self-conscious and really wanted to feel confident, so when I read in a magazine I should look in the mirror and tell myself over and over again, *I am confident,* I was very keen to try it. Unfortunately, every time I repeated the phrase, a voice in my head said, *No you're not; you're not confident at all and you never will be.* I still clearly remember tears rolling down my cheeks as the words I said just reinforced the fact that I was far from confident and made me feel much worse than I had in the first place.

● ●

You've been criticising yourself for years and that hasn't worked. Try affirming of yourself and see what happens. ~ Louise Hay

I now understand that it's asking a lot to expect your mind to accept such far-fetched suggestions when you know deep down that you're lying to yourself. After all the years spent repeating negative messages to yourself, you're more likely to reject positive statements and feel frustrated for trying to convince yourself of something that you know isn't true, as I did.

I find that a far more gentle and effective way of using affirmations is to start off the phrase with *I choose.* If you've been feeling inferior, a failure, or unlovable for most of your life, saying things like *I'm amazing, I can achieve whatever I put my mind to,* or *I love myself just as I am* — wonderfully positive statements that they may be — they're just not going to cut it! However, if you say instead *I choose to know that I'm amazing, I choose to believe I can achieve whatever I put my mind to, I choose to love myself just as I am,* provided they are things that you really choose to think, feel, believe or know, then you're speaking the truth and your subconscious mind will begin to accept those statements as being true.

There's also something about saying *I choose* that's very empowering as you're telling yourself that you're now taking control and giving yourself permission to make positive choices and changes. After repeating your "I choose" affirmations for a while, you're likely to get to the stage where you feel ready to drop the prefix and go straight into the affirmation. Even if you haven't quite reached the stage where you believe it 100%, you're feeling more comfortable saying it and no longer rejecting it.

It's important to state your affirmations in positive terms, saying what you want, rather than saying what you don't want. When you say things like *I don't want to fail* or *I don't want to feel nervous*, your mind doesn't pick up on the 'don't', it just processes *want to fail* or *want to feel nervous*. When I say to you, *Don't think about a blue cow,* what happens? I'll bet you're thinking of a blue cow...and the more I say, *Don't think of a blue cow,* the more you will. If I

"It's important to state your affirmations in positive terms, saying what you want, rather than saying what you don't want."

really want you to stop thinking about that blue cow, I need to ask you to think about something else so that your attention is turned away from a blue cow rather than to it.

So now, think about a pink elephant. Keep thinking about and seeing the pink elephant. Right, now don't think about the pink elephant... Still thinking about it? Can you see how whether I say *think about* something, or *don't think about* something, your attention is drawn to that something. It's a bit like typing into the Google images search box — I don't want to see pictures of red poppies — you're going to get a page full of red poppy photos! So always put into your affirmations whatever it is that you want to focus on or achieve, not the things you don't want.

Flying Lesson 3:
Create your own Effective Affirmations

Take out your journal or notebook and, using the suggestions above on how to create *effective* affirmations, write down some affirmations that feel right for you. Start by thinking about just what you choose to feel, believe or do and create your personalised *I choose* phrases.

Adding emotion to your words will really enhance the effect and your subconscious mind will be far more likely to take on board what you're saying. You may say the words with enthusiasm, determination, joy or even laughter, but if you just repeat the words blandly, they won't be as effective. Say the affirmations below to yourself, first of all in monotone and then imagine saying them again, with emotion in the appropriate italicised places.

a) I can change my life by changing my thinking. (monotone and dull)
b) I *can* change my life by *changing* my *thinking!* (said with conviction)
c) *I choose to believe* that I *can* change my life by *changing* my *thinking.* (emphasising the fact you're making a positive choice even if you don't yet fully believe it!)

Can you feel the difference?

Start using them as soon as possible and the more often you

repeat them to yourself, the sooner they'll become embedded into your subconscious mind. You can repeat your affirmations silently to yourself at any time throughout the day and preferably as often as possible. If you're alone and in a place where you won't be overheard, say them aloud.

Read them from your journal every morning and every night, write them on sticky notes and place them where you'll see them throughout the day, record them and play back the recording while you're driving, travelling or doing your housework!

By frequently repeating your affirmations, you'll begin to replace the critical voice that's been playing repeatedly in your mind for so many years. Your new recording will help you to start accepting yourself, valuing yourself, believing in yourself, respecting yourself and, ultimately, loving yourself unconditionally. It's only when you learn to love yourself that you can expect, or fully accept, love from anyone else.

So, now the autopilot has been switched off and a new flight plan has been created. It's time for you to take control and move one step closer to boarding your flight to Happiness...

Thoughts

Thoughts

Sometimes those who fly solo have the strongest wings.

Step 3

Who's flying the plane?

Taking Responsibility

In Step 1 you learned about how your mind has become negatively programmed with self-doubts, fears and limiting beliefs, and how they've been holding you back. In Step 2 you learned how you could begin to set yourself free from fear and negativity by creating a new plan and reprogramming your mind with positive thoughts and beliefs. Now it's time for the next step by taking full responsibility and committing to make the changes you want to make.

"You have the power to change your life by deciding where you want to get to and then doing what it takes to get you there."

You have the power to change your life by deciding where you want to get to and then doing what it takes to get you there.

No-one can make you read this book, take this journey or change your life, and no-one can stop you either — not your parents, your past, your partner, your ex-partner, your friends, your work colleagues or anyone else.

There was a time when I gave my power away without realising it, allowing myself to be controlled. I felt I needed permission from others before doing certain things I wanted to do or, often, I just didn't do things in case other people didn't approve. As I mentioned in the last chapter, I learned to become self-conscious and worried about what other people might think. I was afraid of displeasing people, I didn't speak up for myself, I let people make decisions for me and I often went along with things even though I really wanted to do something different.

Looking back now from a place of self-empowerment, it's hard to imagine myself ever being so weak but, of course, I'd become conditioned to believe I was small and insignificant, and I didn't appreciate my importance or my rights. At the time when I unexpectedly became

"You need to put on your own oxygen mask before attempting to help anyone else..."

a single parent with two young children to support physically, emotionally and financially, I realised that I had to find the strength to deal with the situation in which I'd found myself.

As an air stewardess I'd been telling passengers for years, *You need to put on your own oxygen mask before attempting to help anyone else,* and I realised that this was what I needed to do. It was time to look after myself, become stronger, start taking responsibility for my life and make my own choices and decisions;

by doing this I'd be doing what was best for my children.

It didn't happen overnight and it was often a difficult journey, spanning several years, but step-by-step, I reclaimed more and more of my power, took control of my life and eventually reached a place where I discovered happiness from within myself. If I'd know then what I've since learned — and am sharing with you in this book — it would have been a much easier and faster process!

• •

Several months after my plane crash, I decided it was time to overcome my negative view of educational institutions and looked into the courses available at the local college. Fortunately, at that time adult education courses were provided free for those who were not in receipt of an income and wanted to train in new skills. I was drawn towards the psychology course as I'd been interested in how the mind works since my late teens but only took my interest as far as evening classes at that time.

I felt very nervous about the idea of stepping through the door and actually enrolling but I eventually managed to pluck up the courage and sign up. A year later I completed the course with flying colours, despite the dreadful conditions I was living under with my ex at the time! This gave me the courage to enrol on a three-month 'Introduction to Counselling' course, although I still lacked the confidence to believe I would be able to go forward and train to be a qualified counsellor.

"Feel the Fear and do it Anyway."

Several months earlier a friend had recommended that I read

the best-selling self-help book, 'Feel the Fear and do it Anyway' by Susan Jeffers. Back then I was still licking my wounds and wasn't ready, but by this time I was beginning to feel a little stronger and my wings had begun to sprout a little more. I bought it, read it and loved it! I completed all the exercises, bought the 'Feel the Fear' affirmations audio and played it in my car every day until it's messages began to have a positive affect on me.

By the time the one-year Counselling Certificate course was due to begin, I was able to feel the fear and enrol anyway...even though my voice trembled when I had to stand up and introduce myself to the group! The course was intentionally very challenging and I was on an emotional roller coaster for the duration of that year, but I completed it and passed all my assignments. Although I'd already taken some great strides forward, I still had reservations about continuing on to the next step, the two-year Counselling Diploma course.

My inner-critic was still trying to tell me that everyone else in the group was worthy of taking the next step, but not me. Thankfully, having begun to take responsibility for my life, I refused to allow that voice in my head to take control. I went ahead and had an interview with my tutor, who told me that she had faith in my ability to become a fully qualified counsellor and she encouraged me to enrol on the next course.

As well as learning how to become an effective and empathic counsellor, an important part of the diploma course focused greatly on self-awareness and personal growth. Each week there was a personal development group and I was required to keep a journal to record my thoughts, feelings, setbacks and achievements from the beginning of the course to the end.

At the end of the two years, while using my journal to reflect upon my development before writing my final essay, I could not believe that the 'small' person with the baby wings who'd started writing in it was the same person who had completed it, and whose wings had grown considerably. This is why I encourage you to keep your own journal as you move forward along your journey. By doing so you'll be able to look back in the future and reflect on your own growth and achievements.

• •

During classes, one of the tutors on the counselling course used to frequently ask, in her strong North Manchester accent, *Who's driving the buz?* The answer she was looking for was always, *The client's driving the buz!* When she first asked the question I had no idea what she was talking about, but I very soon realised that buz meant bus and that she was using a metaphor to

"Who's flying your plane?" say that as counsellors we were meant to enable our clients to take responsibility for themselves and be in control of their own lives. She could just as easily have asked, *Who's flying the plane?,* which is the question I'd like to ask you now... Who's flying your plane?

You may be able to relate to some of my life experiences or perhaps you've always believed you were a product of your circumstances and had no control over how you felt or where you were going in life. You may have been led to believe that your life was

"Now is the time for you to reclaim your power and move from being a Victim to being a Victor!"

mapped out for you and that your destiny was predetermined, but the truth is, no matter in which situation you find yourself, you always have a choice as to how you react. You are not a victim and, unless you choose to relinquish your power to someone else, your life is in your control. Now is the time for you to reclaim your power and move from being a Victim to being a Victor!

As well as learning to take responsibility for the choices and decisions I make in my life, I've also learned to accept responsibility for my feelings. Like so many people, I often used to blame others for the way that I felt, saying things like *He really upset me when he did that* or *She made me so angry when she said that.* Along my journey, I learned that no-one can *make* you feel anything. People may do things that you don't like or agree with, they may be critical or harsh, and you may feel angry or upset, but how you react depends on your own personal beliefs and life experiences. Let me give you an example...

Imagine the scenario: You're sitting in the departure lounge at the airport along with lots of other people waiting to board a regular charter flight. Someone walks past, looks over and loudly makes a sneering remark about the 'commoners' who can't afford to travel first class. Now, some of the people sitting there are going to feel insulted, angry and may even feel they want to punch that person for offending them, some will feel inferior, upset and hurt by the comment, some will laugh in disbelief that someone could be so arrogant, and others may just continue reading their magazine, completely unaffected by the words they'd heard.

Take a moment and think about how you would have reacted.

Then think *why* you would have reacted that way.

Next think how would you like to react in such a situation?

That imaginary pompous individual did not have the power to create anger, upset, amusement or indifference; people reacted according to what was going on inside each of them. If you have a fragile sense of self or you lack self-esteem and believe you're inferior, you're likely to react to such a remark by feeling angry, hurt or both, but if you feel secure and comfortable with yourself, you're more likely to find the remark vaguely amusing or of no significance. Similarly, if someone says to you *Don't be stupid* and you know you're certainly not stupid, you won't take it seriously, but if you grew up being called stupid at home or at school, even though you're an intelligent person, the remark will press a button within you and your feelings will be hurt. Get the idea?

No-one can make you feel
inadequate without your consent.
~ Eleanor Roosevelt

When you take things personally, rather than understanding that other people's opinions, preferences, expectations and reactions are all about them and not about you, you can easily make yourself feel unhappy. Whatever anyone thinks of you is their business, not yours. If you go for an interview and you're not chosen for the job or if someone you like doesn't ask you for a second date, it doesn't mean you're not good enough. We all have preferences and if you're not considered to be the most suitable person for a particular job or the most compatible partner for someone, don't beat up on yourself. Accept that it wasn't meant to be, move on, and find the job or partner that is right for you.

Something else that can lead to your unhappiness is making negative assumptions. Instead of second-guessing what others are thinking or feeling and causing yourself to feel bad, learn to communicate and ask questions. Clarify what's going on; the chances are that you're wrong and causing yourself unnecessary unhappiness by imagining things that are untrue. As you continue to reprogramme your mind and start to love and respect yourself, other people's opinions really won't matter any more. It's so freeing when you no longer care about what other people think of you and you are happy with yourself.

To help yourself become more self-aware, whenever you have a negative reaction to anything someone says or does, just notice how you are feeling and ask yourself, "What is it in me that caused me to react in

"Happiness really is an inside job."

that way?" It's very empowering! If you have 'buttons' that

can be pressed, they're your buttons and you need to decide whether you want to keep them or not. Just as no-one can make you feel inferior without your consent, no-one is responsible for your unhappiness and no-one is responsible for your happiness. Happiness really is an inside job.

In my experience, the fastest and most effective way of releasing those buttons you've let other people press in the past is with an energy psychology therapy known as Emotional Freedom Technique. I first discovered this technique, also known as EFT or Tapping, towards the end of 2005, before it was widely known about in the UK.

EFT was derived from the ancient Chinese healing method of acupuncture; both work by balancing the flow of life force energy through the invisible energy lines, known as meridians, which run through the body. However, unlike acupuncture, which involves inserting very fine needles into specific points all over the body, EFT involves tapping with your finger tips on eight specific points on the face and upper body. Because of this it's very easy to learn and can be used as a self-help tool.

While tapping, you need to focus on your unwanted emotion, belief or issue to bring it to the surface and then release it. The tapping causes electromagnetic vibrations to pass through the connective tissue to the parts of the brain related to emotions, known as the amygdalae. When this happens, relaxing delta brainwaves are increased, the unwanted emotions are decreased and, eventually, they are completely released, usually within a very short space of time.

The energy referred to in EFT is also known as chi, qi, or ki, as in Tai-Chi and Qi-gong (both ancient Chinese practices which combine slow, deliberate movements, meditation and breathing exercises), and Rei-ki, the popular healing method which originated in Japan. Just like electricity waves, energy vibrations can't be seen, but they can be felt and are just as real.

EFT can be used to resolve mental, emotional and physical problems. It can quickly release feelings of stress, anxiety, anger and sadness, and create feelings of calmness and peace. It can also be used to balance

"EFT can be used to resolve mental, emotional and physical problems."

blood pressure, release stress-related aches, pains and other conditions. There have even been cases reported where people have healed themselves from illnesses considered to be incurable, such as Multiple Sclerosis and Cancer.

To learn how to use EFT on long-standing or deep-rooted issues, I'd suggest that you initially work with a therapist who is qualified in this technique, as often the surface problem or limiting belief stems from something of which you're not consciously aware. However, at times you may feel that you do know where your negative feelings or beliefs originated and in those circumstances you can certainly try it for yourself, using the instructions for The Basic EFT Choices Method at the end of this chapter.

No matter what the situation, remind yourself, I have a choice. ~ Deepak Chopra

Soon after studying EFT founder Gary Craig's DVD training on how to use the technique, I received an email asking me to give a talk to a group of people in a large government-run organisation. They wanted me to speak about 'The Power of Positive Thinking', which by that time had become my favourite topic and something I could talk about enthusiastically for hours...informally!

Although my confidence had grown considerably by this time, the very thought of standing up in front of a large group of people instantly filled me with dread. Those early childhood feelings I'd experienced when I believed everyone was looking at me and judging me, and the way I'd felt while being humiliated on stage in front of the whole school assembly were subconsciously triggered when I even thought about being in any situation where all eyes were on me.

My instant reaction was to politely decline but something stopped me and I decided that, once again, I was going to feel the fear and say yes anyway! However, after I'd accepted the invitation, my fear started to grow as the inner critic in my head kept telling me I couldn't do it, I wasn't good enough, people wouldn't be interested in what I had to say, I'd panic and forget what I wanted to say and so on. I began to feel sick with anxiety whenever I thought about giving the talk, so

I decided I'd try this new technique for myself.

Before I started tapping, I estimated that on a scale of one to ten, with ten being the highest it could be, my fear was a nine. After my first three rounds of tapping, the fear had gone down to an eight and, within twenty minutes of tapping, when I thought about giving the talk I had no fearful reaction whatsoever. I was absolutely amazed to find that I just couldn't get that familiar fearful feeling even when I tried hard. I decided I'd keep tapping every day up to the day of the talk

"You can leave behind your unwanted 'excess baggage' and take off on your flight to Happiness..."

until I was certain that the fear had gone, but when I tried to get it back the following day so I could continue to tap it away, it was nowhere to be found!

Since that time I've used this technique with hundreds of clients and watched them release their (often long-standing) issues within a very short period of time. Until you use EFT for yourself, it's difficult to comprehend just how powerful it can be, but once you've experienced it's effects, you're more than likely to want to use it again and again.

Using EFT will put you in the pilot's seat and in control of your emotions, no longer allowing them to control you. You can leave behind your unwanted 'excess baggage' and take off on your flight to Happiness...

Flying Lesson 4:
The Basic EFT Choices Method

I generally prefer to use the EFT Choices Method created by Dr. Patricia Carrington and shared by Gary Craig on his website. To use this method, start by thinking about what it is that you need to release in order to create emotional freedom for yourself. Write down a list of any specific fears, insecurities, regrets, blame, anger, sadness or limiting beliefs and then start to create your own 'set-up phrases' to repeat to yourself while you tap.

The first part of your phrase should begin with *Even though*, followed by the problem you want to release. For example, you may state *Even though I don't feel I deserve to be happy, Even though I need other people to approve of me, Even though I don't believe I'll ever be successful.* The only time I suggest that you put all your attention on what you don't want to feel is while you are tapping, because that's how it works! By focusing on the unwanted feeling you bring it to the surface and then release it.

For the next part of the phrase, you need to create an affirmation about how you'd like to think or feel instead of the way you currently do. In Dr. Carrington's method, the affirmation is preceded with the words *I choose.* As I explained in Step 1, this makes the affirmation that follows more acceptable to your subconscious mind. So, you may say, *I choose to believe that I deserve happiness, I choose to value and approve of myself, I choose to believe in myself and know I can succeed.*

When I tapped on my fear of speaking to an audience, I used the phrase *Even though I feel terrified about giving the talk, I choose to feel calm, relaxed and confident.*

Once you've created the set-up phrase you're going to use, follow the instructions below.

1. Start by asking yourself, on a scale of 0-10, how intense your unwanted feeling or belief currently is, or imagine you're in a situation where you would normally experience your unwanted feeling and recall or imagine the intensity.

2. Using the fingertips of either hand, tap on the karate point at the outside edge of opposite hand, think of the problem and repeat your set-up phrase three times: *Even though I..... I choose to...*

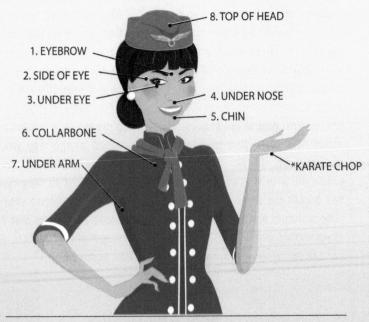

8. TOP OF HEAD

1. EYEBROW

2. SIDE OF EYE

3. UNDER EYE

4. UNDER NOSE

5. CHIN

6. COLLARBONE

7. UNDER ARM

*KARATE CHOP

3. Round 1 - Tap on each point as shown on the diagram, starting at no.1 at the inside corner of either eyebrow and repeat the Negative Reminder Phrase e.g. *I don't feel worthy of happiness*, *I have this fear of speaking in public*. Then take a deep breath down into your abdomen and release it very slowly.

4. Round 2 - For this round repeat just your Positive Reminder Phrase at each point, the *I choose* phrase, e.g. *I choose to believe I do deserve happiness* or *I choose to feel calm, relaxed and confident*. Take another deep breath and release.

5. Round 3 - Alternate the negative and positive reminder phrases. Use your negative reminder phrase for the first point at the inner corner of your eyebrow, then the positive reminder for the second point at the outside corner of our eye, and so on, alternating negative and positive statements for the entire round. Again, follow with a slow, deep breath down to your abdomen and slowly release.

6. At the end of the three rounds, check within yourself again what number of intensity you'd give the unwanted feeling, then continue repeating the three rounds of tapping until the feeling, belief, or problem has gone.

If you don't experience a noticeable change within a few rounds it could be that the phrase you are using isn't quite right or you are not being specific enough about how you feel. For example, rather than stating *I don't deserve to be happy*, it could be that you actually need to release the belief of *I'm not good enough* or *I feel guilty about...* (perhaps something you regret from the past).

If the negative feeling is really emotionally charged or deep-rooted, you may like to complete a few rounds of tapping while just repeating the negative part of the statement to yourself and then move on to the *I choose* part of the phrase when you feel more ready to do so.

As you tap you may feel inclined to say whatever comes into your mind, providing it's relevant to the problem you're aiming to release. The more you're focused on your feelings, the more quickly you'll be able to release them. Continue tapping and focusing until the feeling or belief has gone right down to zero. Once this happens, if you try to get the feeling back and you can't, it's gone for good.

You may find that as one feeling subsides another one comes up, in which case you create a new set-up phrase and start again by focusing on the new unwanted feeling. For example, you might be feeling angry with someone, then as the anger subsides you may start to feel hurt. Each time a feeling is released, become aware of what you're then feeling and, if it's anything negative, create a new phrase that includes that feeling.

As well as visiting Gary Craig's website (www.emofree.com) for further information on traditional EFT, I also recommend that you check out Nick Ortner's website (www.thetappingsolution.com) to learn about alternative variations of tapping.

Life is full of ups and downs so even when you've dealt with the buttons and baggage from the past, something can happen unexpectedly to throw you off balance. When you have this wonderful tool in your box, you can quickly restore equilibrium and deal with the situation in a calm and rational way. It's now time to take the next step and develop a deeper sense of inner peace and calm by learning how to be mindful rather than mind-full...

Thoughts

Thoughts

Thoughts

You cannot be both unhappy and fully present in the Now.

~ Eckhart Tolle

Step 4

A Tranquil Travel Experience

Mindfulness

After learning how to use EFT in Step 3, you now have a tool for life. You are equipped to take responsibility for any unwanted feelings and create emotional freedom by tapping them away. You're leaving your heavy baggage behind and you're travelling light. It's time to take your seat, fasten your seat belt and prepare for take off. All you need to do is relax and go with the flow as you soar up through the clouds and into the clear blue sky above.

Once you've taken off you can't turn around and go back to the past and neither can you propel yourself into the future. You are where you are, encapsulated in the present, experiencing your journey one moment at a time. Unlike animals, the majority of humans are rarely fully present; instead we spend most of our time either mentally reliving the past or transporting ourselves into the future in our minds.

The fact is, when we're living life through our imagination, we are in a virtual reality and missing out on what's happening in actual reality.

When you stop and think about it, it's perfectly obvious that only the present moment is real, but it didn't occur to me just how infrequently I was living in reality until I read the best selling book, 'The Power of Now' by Eckhart Tolle. Reading this excellent book was an important step along my personal journey and changed my way of thinking and being. I began to fully realise that the past has gone, it no longer exists, and it can only affect you when you choose to carry it with you or spend time revisiting it in your mind.

"When you stop and think about it, it's perfectly obvious that only the present moment is real..."

Although it can be enjoyable to reminisce and recall happy memories at times, replaying memories of experiences which weren't so good leads to emotional pain and feelings of regret, guilt, self-recrimination, blame, anger, resentment and sadness. I often hear clients tell me that they are still carrying a grudge towards someone who they feel 'wronged' them many years in the past. The person they're feeling angry or resentful towards is getting on with their lives, completely unaware of their feelings, and the only person they're hurting are themselves.

By choosing to let go of any anger, resentment, blame or guilt you may be carrying from the past, you can feel free to live in the moment. Going over and over what you wish you'd done or wish you hadn't done in the past, what someone else said or did to you, thinking 'if only' or 'why me' is futile. You can't turn the clock back and change what's happened but you can use your past experiences in a positive way to learn your lessons in life, to grow, and to become stronger and wiser.

Just as the past doesn't exist, neither does the future. The future hasn't happened, it's still to come with all it has to bring. As mentioned in the section on creative visualisation in Step 2, when you spend time imagining things going wrong in your life, worrying about all the 'what ifs' — What if I lose my job? What if my partner leaves me? What if I become ill? What if I lose all my money? — you create the same feelings within yourself as if those things have already happened and you cause yourself to feel emotional pain. It makes much more sense to visualise and imagine the future being the way you want it to be and move towards creating that reality instead.

Similarly, when you put pressure on yourself by thinking about what you must or mustn't do, should or shouldn't do, or fear what you're going to be unable to do in the future, you cause yourself to feel stressed and anxious. There are no *musts* or *shoulds* we have to act on in life, so stop this self-imposed pressure and ban those words from your vocabulary, replacing them with the word *could*. The words *must* and *should* suggest there's someone forcing you to do something, whereas the word *could* implies you have a choice and — after reading the last chapter, 'Who's Flying The Plane?' — you now know you always have a choice!

Just think about some of the things you've spent time worrying about in the past, which either never actually happened or they turned out so much better than you imagined they would. You put yourself through all that misery for nothing! Worrying is pointless as it doesn't do anything to change the problems you're creating and repeating over and over in your mind, it just takes away the feelings of peace you could be experiencing if you chose to be in the present.

My life has been filled with terrible misfortunes, most of which have never happened.
~ Mark Twain

When you're 'in your head' rather than 'in the now', the thoughts, feelings and reactions you have in the present are being affected by the experiences you've had in the past and your fears about what might happen in the future. Mindfulness is the practice of being fully in the here and now, without allowing yourself to be influenced by thoughts of the past or future.

A thought is just a thought, you don't have to act upon it. You can learn to observe your thoughts as if from a distance instead of identifying with them and allowing them to control you. The more often you

"You can learn to observe your thoughts as if from a distance instead of identifying with them and allowing them to control you."

pause, become still and create gaps in your overactive thinking, the more often you will connect with your true self and be in 'the now'. By putting yourself in the position of being the 'observer', rather than the 'thinker', you create an escape from the negative effects of your inner chatterbox, setting yourself free to enjoy a sense of inner peace and calm.

I remember one day back in that low, post flight crash period of my life, I was having a little weep and feeling very sad, alone and sorry for myself, when suddenly I felt as if I was observing myself from a distance. It was as if the part of me who was watching me crying wanted to comfort the part of me who was distressed. The words *All things must pass* (the title of former Beatle George Harrison's album) came into my mind and as I told myself, *Let the tears flow, you'll get through this and everything will be OK*, I felt a sense of comfort, knowing that it was true.

After following the suggestions in Step 3, you are hopefully now 'flying the plane' metaphorically but, for the moment, imagine yourself as a passenger, sitting comfortably in your reclined seat in the cabin. A smiling stewardess hands you your long-awaited favourite drink and you smile back as you thank her. As you lift your glass or cup to your mouth you inhale slightly, noticing any aroma there may be, then you take a sip. The sensation on your lips and tongue tells you if it's hot, warm or cold then, as the liquid swirls around the inside of your mouth, you become aware of the flavour. Your tongue may inform your brain that it's sweet, sour, bitter or bland and, as you swallow, you feel a sense of pleasure and satisfaction because you are fully present in your activity of drinking. If your mind had been elsewhere, you wouldn't have noticed these details. Just think about how many times in the past you've just swallowed drinks or food without even noticing them going down...

For the rest of your flight you can choose to stay present and enjoy your journey moment by moment. You may be aware of the sounds of people talking, maybe babies crying, the in-flight announcements from the crew, and the sound of the engines, as you allow yourself to develop a deep sense of inner calm and comfort, and experience a tranquil travel experience.

Alternatively, you could allow your mind to take you off to places where you'll have uncomfortable and unpleasant experiences. It could take you into the future, worrying about what might go wrong during the flight, wondering if there are going to be any problems when you arrive at the airport and feeling impatient and agitated about how long it's going to take until you arrive at your destination. Your mind could also take you back into the past, beating yourself up for not deciding to take this flight sooner, regretting other flights you've taken to places that have led to unhappiness, or blaming others for making you unhappy. You can choose to have a tranquil mind or you can choose to have a chaotic one — again, you always have a choice.

Flying Lesson 5:
Mindfulness Reminders

To help you remember to pause and practise mindfulness throughout your day, refer back to the Thought Stopping Exercise in Step 1 (the Rubber Band Technique). If you don't have something to remind you, you're very likely to forget about being mindful and continue to allow your subconscious mind to take over while you get lost in your head.

As well as wearing a rubber band on your wrist, I suggest putting sticky note reminders in various places such as the bathroom mirror, to remind you when you're brushing your teeth, and on the shower door, reminding you to become fully present as the warm water flows down over you skin and your hair, and you feel the softness of your sponge or the bristles of your body brush as you inhale the scent of your favourite soap or shower gel.

Place a notice above the kitchen sink as a reminder to be consciously aware as you wash up, feeling the warm water on your hands, noticing the colours in the soapy bubbles, how the cups and dishes become clean and shiny as you wash away any stains with the cleaning brush, and then watching as the water flows from the tap, rinsing away the soapy bubbles.

Put a sticky note in the car to remind you to be consciously aware while driving. When out walking, feel your feet in your shoes and be aware each time your heel and then your toes touch the ground. Feel the sun or the rain on your skin, the breeze in your hair. Look around you and notice the buildings, the trees, the birds and the people who pass by.

You could set a phone alarm to remind you every hour or two to pause and be present, even if it's just for two or three minutes. Whatever situation you're in, aim to give it your full attention. While working at your job, whatever you're doing, focus your attention in the present rather than thinking about how much work you need to complete before it's the end of the day or what you're going to do after you finish.

When you're with your family, friends or partner, engage with them and give them your full attention instead of allowing your mind to wander off and think about someone or something else, or becoming engrossed in activities on your mobile phone. By being in the present moment you'll also be making more conscious positive choices instead of allowing your subconscious mind to take over and operate from any limiting beliefs you may still be carrying.

As well as practising mindfulness throughout the day to experience peace for short periods of time, you can extend this practice into longer periods of meditation. There are many methods of meditation and you may like to do your own research into the various options by searching on the Internet.

My first experience of meditation came when I was trying to get pregnant and it wasn't happening. I'd heard that by using meditation to feel calm and relaxed, I was more likely to conceive so I looked into it and discovered that Transcendental Meditation (TM) classes were being held locally. I'd heard of this method when it became widely known about in the late 1960's, the days of 'flower power', peace and love, when George Harrison discovered the benefits of meditation and introduced it to the other Beatles. They all travelled to India to study TM with the Maharishi Yogi, changing Western attitudes about Eastern spirituality. Since that time it's continued to be used by people from all walks of life, including stressed businessmen and women searching for a sense of inner peace.

TM is a method that involves repeating a mantra, which is an ancient Sanskrit word meaning mind-instrument. The idea is that by repeating your mantra (word) you disconnect from the busy thoughts that would normally be filling your mind and stay focused. After going to my first class I went home really looking forward to sitting down for twenty minutes' practice, but within just a few minutes I suddenly became aware that my mind had drifted off and the inner chatterbox had taken over. I went back to my mantra but it kept happening again and again and the more frustrated I got with myself, the worse it became!

When I told my meditation teacher (a middle-aged British woman — not a yogi!) about my experience, she told me that this was normal and with regular practice my mind would begin to slow down and get the message. I just wished she'd told me that before so I wouldn't have felt so frustrated, so I'm sharing that piece of information with you now so you'll be prepared should it happen to you.

Some people prefer to enter a meditative state by watching a candle burning and allowing the flickering of the flame to occupy their mind, while others prefer to listen to a recorded guided visualisation to help them switch off the chatter in their minds as they follow the spoken words inviting them to imagine themselves in a place where they feel calm and relaxed.

Whatever method appeals to you, using meditation as a way to quieten your mind is proven to be a powerful and effective way to let go of thoughts and worries and experience the peace and stillness that lies beneath the busy internal

"...meditation has the additional benefits of releasing stress and lowering your blood pressure."

dialogue of your mind. You could start with just five minutes a day and gradually build up to twenty minutes and see how much calmer you begin to feel. As well as helping you to feel calm relaxed and peaceful, meditation has the additional benefits of releasing stress and lowering your blood pressure.

Other mindfulness practices which improve both physical and mental wellbeing are Yoga, Qi Gong, and Tai Chi, which are all ancient Eastern practices...

Yoga originates from India and there are several different types including Hatha yoga, Iyengar yoga, Ashtanga yoga and Bikram yoga as well as a Chinese version sometimes referred to as Taoist yoga. These yoga techniques include physical stretches, poses and breathing methods to achieve calmness, balance, flexibility, strength and improved health.

Qi gong and Tai Chi originate from China and combine gentle, meditative physical movements with breathing techniques, which help stimulate the flow of *qi, chi* or prana, life force or vital energy to improve physical, mental and emotional health. This is the same energy I referred to towards the end of the previous chapter when explaining how Emotional Freedom Technique works to balance the energy flow through the meridians.

If you are depressed you are living in the past. If you are anxious you are living in the future. If you are at peace you are living in the present.

~ Lao Tzu

Flying Lesson 6:
Passing Clouds

Try this simple form of mindfulness meditation, which involves observing your thoughts coming and going in a detached way without identifying with them. Sit in a quiet place where you won't be disturbed, close your eyes and focus your attention inwards. Begin by taking a few slow, deep breaths down into your abdomen, noticing as the air enters and leaves your body, then just allow your breath to flow in and out at it's own natural pace, not forcing anything, just relaxing and observing.

You may soon become aware that your mind has begun to wander. If this is so, just observe your thoughts as if from a distance and visualise or imagine them as passing clouds in the sky. One moment they're there, the next they've passed by. You really don't need to attach any importance to them or allow them to affect you. They are just thoughts and as you disidentify from them and calmly take your attention back to your breathing they will no longer have any power over you and your mind will be free.

When you start to experience life one moment at a time, instead of rushing from one thought to another, one activity to another, your mind going around in circles, you'll begin to feel a sense of peace, calm and balance, and you'll feel so much happier.

If yo-yo dieting and weight are issues for you, using mindfulness with your eating habits can help. How often do you eat without paying attention to what you're eating or how much you're eating? Do you sometimes eat mindlessly, picking at food while doing something else, perhaps while preparing a meal, watching TV or reading a magazine? If so, it's time to become more mindful of your eating habits.

To begin, make your meal look attractive by using different coloured foods and arranging them attractively on a plate. Before you start to eat, inhale the aroma and see if you can identify the fragrance or the spiciness of the different ingredients. When you take a bite, slowly savour the flavour, be aware of the texture and the temperature as you chew slowly and then swallow.

Put down your fork, spoon or finger food while there's food in your mouth and pause between bites to give your mind time to notice when your stomach begins to feel satisfied. When you begin to become more tuned into your body, you'll know when you've had enough and you can then choose to stop eating, rather than carrying on and eating to excess without being aware of doing so.

Thoughts

Thoughts

If you don't like something, change it. If you can't change it, change your attitude.

~ Maya Angelou

Step 5

Your Attitude determines your Altitude

Positive Mental Attitude

Having let go of your baggage with EFT in Step 3 and freeing your mind by practising mindfulness in Step 4, you should be feeling much lighter and calmer. It's time to start flying at a higher altitude and develop a more positive attitude.

The altitude you can reach in life has everything to do with your attitude. It can raise you up and it can bring you crashing down, it can create problems or it can create solutions, it can make you feel happy or it can make you feel miserable.

"Attitudes can be contagious. Is yours worth catching?"

The fact is, it's not what's going on around you that determines how you feel, it's how you react that makes the difference. Your thoughts, beliefs, opinions and expectations create your perception of yourself and others and this, in turn, drives your attitude. Once you understand that only you are responsible for your attitude, you can start to change it, develop a more positive mental attitude, feel happy and transform your whole life. Attitudes can be contagious. Is yours worth catching?

People with a negative attitude are often sullen and grumpy, focusing on what they see as being wrong with the world rather than what's right. They expect things to go badly, look for faults and are seldom satisfied. They tend to criticise and blame others, take things personally and react defensively. They may make sarcastic comments or even be downright nasty. These are quite obviously not happy people!

Negative people give out negative vibrations, or 'bad vibes', and when you're around them for a while it can feel like they're sucking the energy out of you so you begin to feel miserable too. Perhaps there's someone you know who likes to call you so they can indulge in their favourite pastime of complaining about everyone and everything. You see their number come up on your phone and cringe as your finger hovers over the reject button...no-one enjoys being in the company of someone with a negative attitude.

People with a positive mental attitude are optimistic and tend to smile a lot. They expect good things to happen, look for the good in people and appreciate all they have in their lives. They're generally caring and kind, enjoy seeing other people feeling happy, doing well and succeeding. They take full responsibility for their own emotions and generally stay calm and peaceful. They're flexible, accept what can't be changed and go with the flow. I think it's pretty obvious from what I've said that these are happy people! These are people who are a pleasure to be around and can even lift your spirits with the positive energy and good vibrations they give out.

Loving people live in a loving world, hostile people live in a hostile world. Same world.
~ Wayne Dyer

Some people may have a happy disposition because they had a very positive and nurturing upbringing, others may not have been been so fortunate but have realised that it's possible to change and develop a more positive attitude despite their upbringing. Sadly, many people continue to go through life feeling miserable and are completely unaware that when you change the way you think, you can change the way you feel.

"...when you change the way you think, you can change the way you feel."

Your attitude is formed by your beliefs, which can also create self-fulfilling prophecies. In other words, your 'prophecy' about a person or an event is likely to affect your behaviour towards that person or your experience of that event, leading to your expectation being fulfilled. Your behaviour towards others influences their beliefs about you, which then leads to their behaviour towards you, which reinforces your beliefs. Whether this happens conscioulsy or subconsciously, your beliefs and your behaviour is very likely cause your prediction to come true.

If you hold such beliefs as *Life is tough*, *It's a hard world*, *People aren't to be trusted*, *Bad things always happen to me*, *I can't do it* etc., the likelihood is that's what you'll experience. If you expect things to go wrong, people to take advantage of you or that you'll fail, you're likely to act in a way that will lead to this happening, and you may even find yourself feeling strangely satisfied that it's happened because it's confirmed that your expectations were right!

Of course, on the other hand, this means that if you have a positive mental attitude, expect things to turn out well and that people are generally good and trustworthy, you're likely to behave in a way which will create those expectations and fulfill your positive prophecies...

• •

The bit in the middle...

In the first chapter I started by telling you about how I met and married my ex-husband while working as an air stewardess and how this led to the time in my life when my world came crashing down. In the second chapter, I shared with you some of my early church and convent school experiences and how relieved I was to eventually be able to leave school and be free. I'd now like to tell you about some of the events that took me from being unaware that I even had wings to the time when I first began to try them out and rise higher above ground level...

After leaving school, my love of drawing and painting led me to

consider going to Liverpool College of Art but, because my school experiences had contaminated my view of educational institutions, I had a fear of being confined again so I decided against it. My subconscious mind had, of course, been programmed to believe that ultimately my role in life was to get married and have babies. I wasn't considering a long-term career, I just thought I needed a job that would fill in a few years until motherhood. My altitude had been set by my attitude, which had been set by my downloaded beliefs.

Mum thought I should join the Civil Service as it would be a safe, steady office job, but that sounded to me like a life of total boredom! Nan suggested I train to become a hairdresser and even offered to buy me my own salon once I'd qualified. I think the fact that she liked to have her hair 'done' every week had something to do with her generous offer, but it didn't appeal to me at all. However, I did feel strangely drawn to the world of advertising. It sounded fun and exciting and I daydreamed about my creative talents being discovered and then becoming a commercial artist overnight!

Despite my general lack of confidence, I was resourceful enough to go knocking on doors and was very soon offered a job in a small advertising agency in Liverpool city centre. It turned out to be a rather drab environment and far from what I'd imagined so, after a while, I moved on to a bigger agency where I was very quickly promoted to account manager with my own assistant. While I enjoyed the environment and the people I worked with there, my job was still clerical rather than creative and it really didn't inspire me at all. My dreams of being discovered within the glamorous world of advertising soon faded and I started to search for another line of work.

This turned out to be my first step up towards a higher altitude — 453 foot above ground level to be precise! I'd heard that the prestigious new French restaurant, built at the top of a tower in Liverpool town centre, was soon to open. It was aptly named the Tower Restaurant and, as it slowly revolved, diners would be able to enjoy a panoramic view of the city. When I read that they were recruiting staff I applied for a position, which involved both reception duties, and hostessing within the revolving restaurant, and I was offered the job.

The restaurant was beautifully designed, the food was exquisite and a very glamorous female vocalist sang there in the evenings. I loved the atmosphere, especially in the evenings, as it brought back to my mind scenes from those old Hollywood musicals I'd enjoyed watching since childhood. I also loved the variety of meeting different people each day, including local and visiting celebrities, and I enjoyed working varied hours. I realised then that I wasn't a routine nine-to-five office job type of girl and I never was again!

I stayed there for a couple of years but eventually felt it was time to move on, so I went for an interview with a local recruitment agency. As I discussed various options with the female advisor there, I mentioned that I quite liked the idea of working as a ground stewardess at the airport. She immediately asked if I'd considered applying for a job as an air stewardess.

My automatic reaction, based on a combination of my limiting belief that I wasn't 'good enough' and my rather inflated view of what it took to be an air stewardess, was that this was something way out of my reach. Fortunately, the advisor did a good job of building up my self-belief and I filled in an application form, which led to me being offered a place on the next training course.

It was time to spread my wings further and begin to fly, moving

on from being a restaurant hostess 453 feet above the ground to becoming an air hostess flying 30,000 feet in the air!

• •

Attitude and Communication

As well as affecting how you feel, your attitude determines how you communicate with others, verbally and non-verbally. You don't just communicate with the words you say. Your facial expressions, posture, body language and the way you say the words you say can all speak louder than the words you are actually saying.

There are four main types of communication — Aggressive, Passive-Aggressive, Passive and Assertive, and whichever style you use speaks volumes to others about the type of attitude you have and the kind of person you are, and they then respond to you accordingly.

As well as the pessimistic type of negative attitude I've already written about, there are many other types of 'bad attitude'.

Some examples are listed below. See if you can guess into which communication categories you would put each of these personality types:

1. **The Diva:** Superiority complex. Inflated opinion of self. Demanding. Delusional. High Maintenance. Needs to be the centre of attention. Expects everyone and everything to revolve around her. Emotional outbursts if she doesn't get her own way.

Attitude: I'm important. I'm a 'princess'. It's all about ME. My needs and moods are more important than yours. You should pander to me. If I don't get what I want I'll cause a scene.

2. **The Sulker:** Indirect expressions of hostility. Disconnect between words, facial expressions and emotions. Denies true feelings. Pretends to be agreeable while feeling resentful. Doesn't express his needs but feels angry when they're not met. Resentful. Sarcastic. Agrees to do something then takes a long time to do it as 'punishment' to the person he feels resentful towards. Withholds affection. Gives the silent treatment.

    Attitude: If you really cared about me you'd know what I want. I'll say I'm OK but I'm going to suffer in silence. I'm not going to show my true feelings but I'll get even with you in my own way.

3. **The Drama Queen:** Attention seeker. Dramatic highs and lows. Blows things out of proportion. Takes everything personally. Highly strung. Blames others. Causes arguments. 'Falls out' with people easily. Can't let things go. Self-absorbed. Inappropriate hysterical outbursts. Blames others for his feelings.

    Attitude: I'm not happy and it's all your fault. Don't say or do anything to upset me or I'll explode. If things don't go the way I want them to I'll be very angry. I need to let everyone know how angry I am.

4. **The Victim:** Inferiority complex. Feels sorry for herself. Sympathy seeker. Doesn't accept responsibility. Blames others for circumstances and feelings. Keeps going over old

stories. Dwells on the past.

Attitude: It's not fair. I'm unlucky. Poor me. I'm a martyr. Nothing works out for me. People take advantage of me and let me down. It's all their fault. I can't change my life. I need someone to save me. I'm powerless. Why does it always happen to me?

5. **The Know-it-all:** Self-important. High opinion of himself. Believes he's an expert on everything. Tries to belittle others. Dogmatic. Egocentric. Stubborn. Talks over people. Frequently interrupts. Often loud. Overpowering. Closed-minded.

Attitude: I'm not listening. I'm not interested in what you think. I'm right and you're wrong. My knowledge is superior. The truth doesn't matter if it doesn't match my beliefs.

Underlying all of these types of attitudes are feelings of insecurity and an inability to take responsibility for creating their own happiness. They are all self-centred and have a neediness, whether it's for other people's attention, admiration, adoration, sympathy, or to 'make' them feel good and they all take things personally.

Have you identified which communication category each one fits into? The Drama Queen, The Diva and The Know-it-all act as if they are in some way superior. They are manipulative and generally tend to communicate in an *aggressive* way, which helps them feel powerful — which they're not — and consequently less insecure.

The Sulker acts in a *passive-aggressive* way, feeling *aggressive* but unable to express it outwardly, and The Victim acts in a *passive* way, feeling powerless. Both of these types are also manipulative in their own way.

It's impossible to climb to a higher altitude of happiness while having a negative attitude. Happy people communicate in an *assertive* way. They are honest and able to express their needs and opinions calmly and confidently and have no need to act defensively or aggressively. They don't act as though they are superior or inferior; they are comfortable with who they are. They value themselves enough to say *No* without feeling guilty and they don't take advantage of other people or try to manipulate them. They don't need other people to make them feel good as they value and respect themselves. They take full responsibility for their own feelings and circumstances, and are in control of their own lives. These are people who it's a pleasure to be around and whose presence lifts you up higher rather than dragging you down.

"It's impossible to climb to a higher altitude of happiness while having a negative attitude."

Just as in any other situation where you're working as part of a team, the attitude of the individuals who make up the cabin crew on a flight has a big impact on the experience of the flight. While I was an air stewardess there were times when I had to work with melodramatic 'drama queen' types who over-reacted and made it a major issue if there was a delayed take off or there were lots of children on a flight.

There were the self-important 'divas' who acted as though they were doing the airline a favour by working for them; they complained they were missing out on their social lives because they had to work unsociable hours, they didn't like wearing a uniform, or the crew meals didn't meet their standards. There were also the self-pitying 'victims' who imagined they were always given the worst trips while everyone else got the good ones, the 'sulkers' who resented being asked to carry out duties and sighed or rolled their eyes, but would never actually admit that they had a problem, and the 'know-it-alls' who tried to tell everyone how they should be doing things. Interestingly, they would also often complain about the bad attitudes of passengers while seemingly oblivious to their own!

Fortunately, the majority of the crew members I flew with were much more positive and would generally arrive for a flight smiling and enthusiastic. They embraced the fact that rosters vary from month to month and if they weren't allocated the flights they were hoping for that month, they very soon would be. They were thankful they didn't have to buy special work clothes or even think about what to wear for work and they appreciated that being provided with free meals and drinks was a bonus and saved them money. They happily accepted that flying in the evenings and weekends was a necessary part of working for an airline, just as in any other jobs which provide a round-the-clock service, and considered themselves very fortunate to have a career which involved travelling to places they would normally have been unlikely to visit.

We all did the same job, yet some focused on what they didn't like, looked for problems and made themselves feel miserable, while others focused on the many benefits of the job which led to them feeling happy. It all depended on each individual person's attitude. It was of course so much more enjoyable having smiling, helpful,

"You can't change other people's attitudes, but you can change your own..."

positive people to work with in the cabin crew and I'm sure they made the passengers' experience so much more enjoyable too!

I imagine you've come across people with similar attitudes to those I've mentioned, either in personal relationships or work situations. In fact there may be some of these types of people in your life at the moment. It's likely that you've also come across some other types of bad attitudes too, including rude, 'can't be bothered' shop assistants who carry on talking to colleagues while you wait to be served, abrupt servers in bars and restaurants who don't even make the effort to look at you as they serve you, and surly, officious front desk staff at hotels, libraries and doctor's surgeries. You can't change other people's attitudes, but you can change your own and choose not to let their negativity affect you.

As far as possible, surround yourself with people who are going to lift you higher and aim to avoid the company of people whose negative energy will drag you down. If you usually spend your time in the company of friends who tend to gossip, look for faults in others and generally focus on the negatives, it's time to seek out the company of more positive people and make some new friends. Meanwhile, it's far better to be alone than in bad company.

If there are pessimistic, complaining, critical people in your life who you can't completely avoid, such as work colleagues or family members, refuse to allow yourself to get involved in their negative conversations and make an effort to change the subject to a more uplifting one. It can help to imagine yourself surrounded by an invisible protective bubble of positive energy which keeps out their negative vibes. You'll find that the more you do this, the more real it will feel. As you start to develop a more positive attitude, you may well find that you start to have a positive effect on those people who are around you.

It helps to avoid watching or listening to bad news. Most of the reported news is negative and gives the impression of a bad, bad, world. The truth is there are so many positive, happy and wonderful things going on in the world, they're just not often reported. When a negative news report suddenly appears on TV or you're driving along listening to music on the radio and suddenly you find your mood sinking as you hear about a stream of negative, distressing events – switch off!

Don't worry that you won't know what's going on in the world, you'll hear what you need to from other people or through social media. Listening to a condensed report of one negative event after another does not give you a balanced view of what's going on in the world, it gives you an unrealistic view of the world being a terrible place.

Flying Lesson 7:
Self Reflection

Take some time to reflect on any aspects of yourself you recognised in the personality types mentioned in this exercise (The Diva, The Sulker, The Drama Queen, The Victim and The Know-it-All) and in the ways of communication (Aggressive, Passive-Aggressive, Passive and Assertive).

If you've become aware of some traits you dislike, don't berate yourself or feel bad, remember you weren't born that way, you've unintentionally been programmed by other people and you're now in the process of being re-programmed — by yourself!

Without blaming anyone else, think about some specific situations where you've acted or reacted in a negative way, sending out 'bad vibes', whether verbally or non-verbally.

Remembering that you are now taking full responsibility for your actions and reactions, write down the details of your interaction in your journal or notebook.

Spend some time thinking about how you could have reacted in a more positive way and write down some alternative behaviours you now choose to adopt and use in the future.

If you've become aware that you need to work on developing a more positive attitude, be honest with yourself about the personality traits you need to change.

To help encourage you to make these changes, focus on how they will affect your life for the better — in your relationships, your family life, your social life and your career or business.

Feel grateful that you've had a wake-up call and you can now begin using your new awareness and the tools I'm sharing in this book to change your old attitude for a more positive one that will help you continue on your flight to Happiness.

Life is so much more enjoyable when you have a positive mental attitude and without one you can't be truly happy. If you believe you can change your attitude, then you will be able to. Remember the Henry Ford quote in Step 1? *If you think you can or you think you can't, you are right...*

If you need to remind yourself of how you can change the thoughts and feelings that have been creating your negative attitude, refer back to the Thought Stopping exercise at the end of Step 1, the NLP Anchor Technique at the end of Step 2, the EFT Tapping technique at the end of Step 3 and the Mindfulness techniques in Step 4. Now it's time to move on to Step 6 and begin to appreciate the many things you have to be thankful for!

Thoughts

Thoughts

The Greatest Source of
Happiness is to be grateful
at all times. ~ Zig Ziglar

Step 6

Appreciation of Aviation... and everything else!

Gratitude

In Step 5 we looked at the importance of creating a positive mental attitude in order to feel happy. Now, in Step 6 we're going to look at the importance of developing a very specific type of positive attitude, an attitude of gratitude. Gratitude is a powerful key towards creating happiness from the inside.

The default mode for the majority of people is to take for granted what they have and focus more on what they want but don't have. Having an attitude of gratitude involves feeling a sense of appreciation and thankfulness for all we have and all we experience in our lives. It's not possible to feel a true sense of gratitude and feel unhappy at the same time, so if you want to feel happier, it's time to start feeling more thankful for the simple little things as well as the bigger ones.

When we travel through life with our minds and our eyes 'closed', much of the time focused on the mundane and the pettiness in our heads, we miss so much. We are often oblivious to the wonders of nature that surround us: the flowers, the trees, the mountains, the valleys, the rivers, the waterfalls, the beaches, the oceans, the birds and the bees and all the other creatures which fly through the skies, as well as those that swim through the seas and walk the earth.

Develop a sense of wonderment and awe. Think about how a mighty oak tree grows from a tiny acorn, wild flowers miraculously appear from tiny cracks between paving stones, a furry caterpillar spins itself a silky cocoon and emerges as a beautiful butterfly, tadpoles lose their tails and grow legs to become frogs, birds migrate by following the stars and the earth's magnetic field to reach their destination.

If you're already practising mindfulness, having read Step 4, you'll find that when you're fully present you are aware of the reality of your surroundings and all there is to be thankful for and can feel an immense sense

"When you pause and look towards the sky, really look, it's impossible not to feel a sense of awe and wonder at its magnificence."

of gratitude. When you pause and look towards the sky, really look, it's impossible not to feel a sense of awe and wonder at its magnificence.

Feel a sense of appreciation for the shifting shapes of the passing clouds, the rainfall, rainbows, snowflakes, sunshine, sunrise, sunsets, the waxing and waning of the moon, and the galaxies of stars. Being aware that you are gazing out from planet earth, spinning around the sun at a speed of 1040mph along with all the other planets of the solar system, makes it even more awesome!

Apart from the wonders of nature, how often do you stop to appreciate the many wonders of science and technology? Most of you reading this book will be able to just flick a switch and access electricity to light, heat or cool a room, cook, chill or freeze food, power your devices and watch a choice of programmes and movies on TV. Through the amazing Internet you can access information on just about anything you want to know, share information and talk to people all over the world, and you can do this wirelessly on laptops, tablets and smartphones. Even if you don't have your own gadgets, you can access computers at libraries without charge. You can turn a tap and clean, fresh water will flow out instantly for you to drink, wash and clean with. When you stop to appreciate how very fortunate you are to have all these things, don't you feel truly grateful?

As you're travelling on your flight to Happiness, let's also consider science on a larger scale and pause to appreciate aviation. How amazing is it that a Boeing 747 aircraft weighing 970,000 lb (439,985 kg) can take off from the ground and fly thousands of miles through the sky? As the aircraft builds momentum and takes off, it lifts from the ground and the law of gravity is defied as the law of aerodynamics allows it to soar up into the air.

How often do you stop to think about and appreciate the fact that an aircraft can take you from London to New York, travelling approximately 3,460 miles (5,568 kilometres) in around seven hours? Rather than feeling a sense of awe and appreciation at these amazing facts, so many people turn their attention towards the more petty aspects of air travel and find things to complain about.

As you now know, whatever you choose to focus your attention on will create your feelings, your actions and your reactions. If your mind is fixed on finding faults, you'll find them everywhere you go. Remember learning about how you can create self-fulfilling prophecies in Step 5? If you go through life focusing on what you haven't got, you'll continuously feel a sense of lack and feel envious or even resentful of what you see or imagine other people having. Doesn't it make sense to go through life focusing on all the things you have for which you feel thankful?

• •

After the horrendous year of living under my ex-husband's control in the house we built, I was so thankful to eventually move out and have a home where I could lock the door and feel safe, even though it was a temporary home. However, when my short-term rental contract was nearing an end, I had a very real fear about where we were going to live next so in desperation I applied to the local council and asked to be put on their housing waiting list.

One day while my children were at school, I was sitting on my bed feeling a real sense of helplessness and despair when I suddenly found myself crying out and asking for help, although I wasn't sure who I was asking. I knew it wasn't the mythical God I'd seen depicted in paintings in the Catholic church I visited as a child — an old man in the sky with a grey beard, pointing a judgemental finger down at me. However, I sensed there was a powerful presence I could call upon to ask for help. It wasn't until several years later when I read the book, 'Ask and it is Given' by Esther and Jerry Hicks, I reflected over the years that had passed and could clearly see that from that moment, when I cried out and asked for help, help was given.

> "...when I cried out and asked for help, help was given."

A few days after my experience, someone from the council office came out to interview me. After I'd answered all her questions, she paused and looked away for a while as though she was thinking something through and then she looked back at me and told me she knew of a house which would soon be available to rent. It was in a quiet cul-de-sac in a very pleasant residential area nearby and had been refurbished by a housing association. It was going to be offered for a long-term let at a low rental fee.

She said she'd like to put me forward for this house and asked if I'd be interested in it. Interested? I could hardly believe my ears! There must have been so many people on the council waiting lists who would have loved the opportunity to rent a house like this, yet there I was, a brand new applicant, being offered this opportunity. I was so thankful I wanted to cry — this time with joy!

Despite all my losses — the 'loving partner' who I'd believed my ex-husband to be, the father of my children, the dream home we'd designed together, my dreams for the future, emotional security, financial security — I was still able to feel incredibly grateful that my children and I were going to be given the opportunity to live in this three-bedroomed semi-detached house.

It wasn't the beautiful six-bedroomed dream house I'd planned on living in as a complete family, but it was a comfortable home in a safe, secure environment and it was affordable. We lived there for twelve years while the children were growing up and I felt so blessed every day for having been provided with this home at a time when we were almost homeless.

●●●●●●●●●●●●●●●●●●●●●●●●●●●●●●●●●●

*Be thankful for what you have,
you'll end up having more. If you concentrate
on what you don't have, you'll never, ever,
have enough.*
~ Oprah Winfrey

Having had so much and then finding myself with so little helped me to be more thankful for what I did have. Since that time I've continued to be aware of how much I've had to feel grateful and appreciative for: my family, my friends, the roof over my head, the areas I've lived in, the books I've read, the courses I completed, the lessons I learned, the people who came into my life, the personal growth I achieved and the strength I gained. It didn't require any effort on my part to feel a continuous sense of gratitude, it just happened naturally.

I still wake up every morning and immediately feel thankful

for my bed, my duvet, my pillows, my heating in the winter months and my garden in the summer months. Every morning when I go downstairs and walk across the living room to open the curtains, I feel such a sense of appreciation of the lovely home and area in which we now live.

When I walk down the second flight of stairs, I'm so thankful for my ideal office space and therapy room. I love and appreciate the beautiful car that I've bought for myself and, when I'm driving along and see the fields and the parks as well as the shops and the restaurants in the nearby areas, I continuously feel appreciation bubbling up inside me. I can feel it now as I write. There is always so much to be thankful for!

You don't need to have lots of money to appreciate your life. You might not have enough money to go on exotic holidays, buy designer clothes or eat out in fancy restaurants, but you don't need those things to be happy. You can enjoy inexpensive days out in the area where you live, be creative with the clothes you already have and enjoy trying out new recipes at home — I know this from experience!

I managed on a very low income for several years but this encouraged me to be creative and seek out bargains and activities which were free or almost free for the children and I. We'd occasionally go to a burger or pizza restaurant and they'd have a children's meal while I just had a coffee, but it didn't get me down. I appreciated the fact that we were able to do that now and again and felt happy that they were happy. I was extremely grateful for the food parcels Mum and Nan gave me whenever we visited them, the holiday my daughter's godmother provided for us, and the offers of help I received from so many people around that time.

It's likely that you already have a roof over your head, a comfortable bed to sleep in, clothes to wear and food to eat, and you probably have people in your life who you love or at least like, whether partners, family, friends or colleagues. These are all things to be thankful for and happy about every day, yet many people take them for granted and convince themselves that they won't really be happy until they have a pay rise, a designer handbag, a holiday or a new partner.

"When you're truly feeling a sense of gratitude and appreciation, it's impossible to be anything but happy!"

If you're always looking for something new to bring you happiness, it's likely that once you have it you'll begin to take it for granted and start thinking about the next thing you want but don't have. When you're truly feeling a sense of gratitude and appreciation, it's impossible to be anything but happy!

Flying Lesson 8:
Practising Gratitude

Start telling people how much you appreciate them, not by just by politely saying the words "thank you". Say it from your heart and tell them why you are grateful for what they've done or just for having them in your life. Perhaps there's a colleague at work who's really helpful and will always go the extra mile to help you out if you need it, a family member who's always been there to support you when you have a problem, a friend who always helps you see the funny side of things and makes you laugh, but you've never really told them just how much you appreciate them.

If you have a partner or children, don't assume they know you love them, tell them often that you do and tell them what's loveable about them. People love to feel appreciated and valued, so show them your gratitude. It's not happy people who are thankful, it's thankful people who are happy!

> **"It's not happy people who are thankful, it's thankful people who are happy!"**

At the end of each day take out your journal and write down everything you can think of that you're grateful for having experienced during that day. They could be things like having a good chat with a friend, something interesting you read, a walk in the park, the sunshine, a delicious meal, a compliment, music you listened to, something that made you laugh or the fact that you are now beginning to feel a sense of freedom and inner peace.

Every day add more things you feel thankful for so your list will grow longer and longer. Frequently read through your growing list of the many positive experiences and people you're fortunate to have in your life. As you continue to do this, you'll feel the inner glow of gratitude and become happier with each and every passing day.

Practising gratitude soon becomes a habit and when you start to appreciate the good things in your life regularly, you'll not only feel so much happier, you'll give out positive energy vibrations which will attract back to you more things and people to be thankful for. This is known as the Law of Attraction, which we'll be looking at in more depth in Step 7.

Thoughts

Thoughts

Thoughts

If you want to find the secrets of the universe, think in terms of energy frequency and vibration.

~ Nikola Tesla

Step 7

The Physics of Flight

Metaphysics, Quantum Physics and Universal Energy

In the previous six steps, we've been mainly focusing on how to change your thoughts, emotions and attitudes. In this final step I'd like to help you to connect with your spirit and fly to the universe and beyond...

As we travel through this life experience as human beings, we consist of a body, a mind and a spirit, all of which are interlinked. In order to be our best possible selves physically, mentally and spiritually, these aspects of ourselves need to be in balance. We all know that it's much easier to feel happy when our bodies are in good health, fit and free from pain, and when our minds are calm, open and free from turmoil. Similarly, when you're aware of and connected to your spirit, you can feel so much happier — uplifted, inspired, electrified, in high-spirits. Conversely, when you're unaware of or disconnected from your spirit, you're likely to feel low-spirited, uninspired, downhearted, fearful and alone.

Whether you're Buddhist, Jewish, Christian, Hindu, Muslim, any of the other thousands of religions, or you have no religious beliefs at all, you can experience a sense of your spirit. Think about the feeling that flows through you when you feel pure unconditional love for a person or an animal, see a new-born baby, listen to the beautiful sound of a choir singing in perfect harmony, stare up at a starry, moonlit sky at night, see amazing wonders of nature, such as Niagara Falls or the Grand Canyon.

"As you continue to fly through the air on your flight to Happiness, are you ready to allow your spirit to soar?"

There may have been times when you've experienced a deep connection with nature, a true sense of joy, tears in your eyes, a tightness in your throat, a tingle down your spine, a sense of energy flowing through your whole body. I can still clearly remember the feeling of total awe I experienced in my early teenage years, the first time I watched the Red Arrows fly through the sky in perfectly synchronised flight. As you continue to fly through the air on your flight to Happiness, are you ready to allow your spirit to soar?

• •

A couple of years after my crash landing, I was beginning to get off the ground again and was in the second year of my counselling training when I saw an advert in a local paper about a ten-week

Practical Philosophy Course. I read that it would involve looking at metaphysics, the classic philosophies of the East and the West, life and it's meaning, what holds us back and what sets us free.

The course would invite students to apply the words of the wise in daily life, offer practical tools for experiencing greater freedom and happiness, and explore the answer to the question, *Who am I?* It would also look at wisdom and how it's acquired, awareness, consciousness, the power of reason, and the possibility of unity behind everything... and amazingly, apart from a £5 enrolment fee, it was free!

As I read all this, I felt a sense of excitement tingling inside of me; I was intrigued, I wanted to understand more, there were so many questions that I wanted to know the answers to. Enrolling on this course was one of the best decisions I've ever made. Every week, I was fascinated by the content of the session and I felt excited and instinctively knew I was on the right path. Students were encouraged to neither accept nor reject the principles presented in class but to test out their value by applying them to their daily lives. I didn't quite 'get' all of it at first, but as I moved forward, I was able to look back and say to myself, Aaaah, now I understand!

Each week the group facilitator would read out a few words of wisdom, which may have been spoken by Socrates, Einstein, Shakespeare, Jesus, the Buddha or by many other wise and wonderful people who have walked this earth, then members of the group were asked to reflect on what we thought their words meant in more practical terms and a discussion would follow.

During the tea break there was a bookstall selling books on practical psychology, philosophy and self-development. I bought

**some wonderful books there which helped me make more sense
of the new way of thinking I'd begun to discover.**

● ●

Some of the most influential books I read at that time
were 'Awareness' by Anthony de Mello and 'The Road Less
Travelled' by M. Scott Peck, followed by 'A Return to Love'
by Marianne Williamson and 'Love is Letting go of Fear' by
Gerald Jampolsky. The latter two were based on the principles
of 'A Course in Miracles' which I'd bought previously but,
while I found that book quite heavy going, I found that these
books expressed it's lessons in a much simpler way.

Every week my mind and my heart opened more and I felt my
spirit soar. This was one of the most positive life-changing
experiences I have ever had. After completing the ten-week
course, I moved on to the next level for another ten weeks,
and then the next, and this continued for three years. After a
few months, we started meditating as a group and I started
practising regularly at home again. For me it was a period of
great spiritual awakening and growth.

Since that time I've lived my life not just from the knowledge
in my head but from an inner knowing deep inside. This
knowing came from my own experiences and the experiences
and wisdom shared by many enlightened writers, philosophers
and teachers throughout the ages. Their wise words have
stood the test of time and, just as we students of philosophy
were encouraged to neither accept nor reject the principles
presented in class but to test out their value by applying
them to our daily lives, I would recommend that you, as a
student on the flight to Happiness, do the same.

Once I became aware of the invisible universal energy flowing through me, and all around me, I began to open up and allow myself to connect with it and since that time my life has gone from strength to strength. When I look back over the years, I can see that there were so many messages, synchronicities, experiences and people who came into my life and helped me in one way or another. I didn't have a flight plan, yet I strongly sense that I was guided onto the flight path leading to Happiness.

Fast-forward ten years to 2006. I was leaving a Mind, Body Spirit exhibition in Manchester when I heard someone mention a new film that had recently been released on DVD. It was called 'The Secret' and was said to contain enlightening and exciting knowledge. I was intrigued and, after reading more about it later on the Internet, I couldn't wait to get my hands on it. I then read that it was only being sold from one shop in the UK and the shop was in London. It was a Saturday night, so the earliest it could have been posted to me would have been the following Monday, with it hopefully arriving on the Tuesday or Wednesday of the following week.

I just didn't want to wait that long and felt that there had to be a way of getting hold of a copy sooner. I continued searching the Internet with determination and eventually came across the information that the London shop selling the DVD had a stand at the exhibition in Manchester where I'd been that day. I'd browsed a bookstall there but hadn't noticed its name or that it was selling 'The Secret' DVD because I didn't know anything about the film while I was there.

First thing the next morning I went back to the exhibition and later that day I got to watch 'The Secret'. As I listened intently to what the Law Of Attraction experts shared about their own experiences and how we all attract what we focus our attention on, I felt truly inspired. When I heard someone say, *If it worked for me, why wouldn't it work for you?* I instinctively knew that this had to be true...

The film was created by Australian film-maker Rhonda Byrne after she read a book called 'The Science of Getting Rich' by Walter Wattles, published in 1910. In this book she learned about what Wattles referred to as 'a certain way of thinking'. That 'way of thinking' included similar timeless teachings to those I'm

"If it worked for me, why wouldn't it work for you?"

sharing with you in the seven steps of this book: to become aware and mindful of your thoughts, to silence your inner critic and use positive affirmations, to have a positive attitude and practise gratitude, and to visualise and imagine already having what you want in your life in order to attract it.

It taught that by doing these things while living harmoniously with the Universal Intelligence, you would be able to consciously manifest your desires and create the life you want to live. A similar way of thinking and being has been referred to throughout the centuries by some of the world's greatest scientists, artists, authors, sculptors, composers and philosophers, including Einstein, Shakespeare, Galileo, da Vinci, Aristotle and Plato.

Rhonda Byrne was so inspired by the astonishing results she began to experience through practising the lessons in the book, she wanted to share what she'd learned with the world, so she created her film and called it 'The Secret'. Shortly after releasing the DVD, a hard-back book of the same name was published and was endorsed by Oprah Winfrey as being one of her all-time favourite spiritual and psychological books. At the time of writing there are 28 million copies of this book in print.

'The Secret' refers to a universal law known as 'The Law of Attraction', and the main principle of this law is what we send out we attract back. I'd often heard people saying things like *What goes around comes around...Like attracts like...You reap what you sow...* but I didn't think too much about what they actually meant until after watching the film. The Law of Attraction, which from now on I'll refer to as the LOA, teaches that our thoughts create our emotions, something I already knew, but what I wasn't aware of before watching 'The Secret' is that our emotions create our energy vibrations.

"What goes around comes around...Like attracts like... You reap what you sow..."

I'd listened to 'Good Vibrations' by 'The Beach Boys', I'd heard people talk about sensing a 'bad vibe' from someone, or saying they walked into a room and felt they could have 'cut the atmosphere with a knife', or that they really felt a 'connection' with someone, but I hadn't previously given too much thought to what those expressions actually meant.

I began to understand that the LOA was all about the invisible universal energy I've mentioned earlier, which we can't see but we can certainly feel, the energy which connects us to the universe, the same energy, life force, chi, qi, Reiki that I talked about in Step 3 when I wrote about how EFT and the energy system we have within us.

If you've not previously heard of the LOA, please understand that this is not some 'woo-woo' nonsense, this is science, and the energy vibrations we emit can be measured using quantum physics. Quantum physics, also known as quantum mechanics, is a branch of science which explains the nature and behaviour of matter and energy on an atomic and subatomic level.

It tells us that nothing is solid and that everything is made up of energy. Our bodies are made up of tissues and organs, which are comprised of 50 trillion cells, which are made up of molecules, which are made up of atoms, which are made up of sub-atomic particles, which are made up of energy...and they are continuously giving off and absorbing this intelligent energy.

Quantum physicists have scientifically proven that the whole universe is an ocean of intelligent energy and, therefore, we are energetically connected to the universe. Energy vibrations are continuously emitted from and attracted to the atoms in our cells. They travel out into the universe, attracting and connecting with other energy vibrations travelling on a similar frequency, positive vibrations travelling at a higher frequency and negative vibrations at a lower frequency.

> **"Quantum physicists have scientifically proven that the whole universe is an ocean of intelligent energy and, therefore, we are energetically connected to the universe."**

As I learned this I began to become even more aware of just how powerful our thoughts are... I fully realised that, as our thoughts create our emotions and our emotions affect our cells and consequently our energy vibrations, once we replaced our negative thoughts with positive ones, we would automatically begin to emit positive energy vibrations and attract more positive energy back. This meant that we would then create the experiences we want to have in our lives, rather than those we don't want!

I'm very open to new information and ways of increasing my self-awareness and self-development, and it's not always necessary for me to have scientific proof of how things work, just as long as they do. In fact I've always thought that it's very arrogant for mere mortals to say that they don't believe in something just because it hasn't yet been scientifically proven. After all, we humans are tiny dots compared to the vastness of the mysterious universe! However, I've become fascinated with the aspects of quantum physics which relate to universal energy and the LOA and I find it all very exciting!

*Science cannot solve the
ultimate mystery of nature. And
that's because in the last analysis, we ourselves are
a part of the mystery that we are trying to solve.*

~ Max Planck
(Nobel Prize winning founder of quantum physics)

If you're interested in learning more about quantum physics and the LOA in an uncomplicated way, I recommend the series of 'Why Quantum Physicists...' books and e-books by Greg

Kuhn, often referred to as 'The Law of Attraction Science Guy'. When I first read them a couple of years ago, they really helped me to gain a clearer understanding of these fascinating topics.

I'd also recommend 'The Honeymoon Effect' in which one of my favourite authors, Bruce Lipton PhD, provides an excellent explanation of quantum physics and those energy vibes I've been talking about. He also explains just how our subconscious programming can cause us to unwittingly sabotage our relationships and how reprogramming our minds through mindfulness, hypnosis and energy therapies, such as EFT Tapping, can enable us to create happy, healthy relationships.

Some of my other favourite authors who combine science, self-help and spirituality in their books include Wayne Dyer PhD, David Hamilton PhD, Dr. Deepak Chopra, Dr. David Hawkins and Dr. Joe Dispenza. I've listed some of their books, along with those from other authors, in the 'Flight Manuals' (Resources) page at the back of this book.

It was soon after watching 'The Secret' in 2006 that I read the book, 'Ask and it is Given' by Esther and Jerry Hicks, the couple whose LOA seminars played an important part in the making of the original DVD of 'The Secret'. Although I found this book fascinating, it wasn't until the beginning of 2015 that I was fully ready to appreciate Esther's sharing of the wise teachings of 'Abraham'. This came after watching several online videos of Esther answering questions from a live audience with her downloaded wisdom, wit and clarity.

To learn more about Esther Hicks and the teachings of

'Abraham', I recommend that you visit www.abraham-hicks.com as well as searching YouTube for Abraham-Hicks videos.

*A human being is a part
of the whole, called by us the universe,
a part limited in time and space. He experiences
himself, his thoughts and feelings as something
separated from the rest, a kind of optical
delusion of his consciousness.*

~ Albert Einstein

● ●

As I watched 'The Secret' and listened to the experts talk about how they'd used these methods to create their achievements and successes, I began to realise that I'd already used the LOA more than twenty years earlier, although it wasn't referred to by that name at the time. Somehow over the years I'd forgotten about using what I'd learned, but back in the mid-eighties I'd read two books which led me to create something I wanted more than anything else in the world — 'Bring out the Magic of Your Mind' by Al Koran and 'Creative Visualisation' by Shakti Gawain.

Six years before the 'plane crash', after four years of marriage, four house moves, four pets (two cats and two dogs), about fourteen trips overseas and various fertility tests and treatments, there were still no babies and I was feeling unfulfilled. I took up yoga, did the Transcendental Meditation course I mentioned in Step 4 and meditated daily. I even started going back to church and praying.

When I read 'Bring out the Magic of Your Mind', I began to learn about the untapped power of our minds and the powerful magnetic energy we can use to create what we want in our lives. I felt so excited, as if I'd woken up from a dream, and I started to put into practice the lessons from the book.

These lessons led me to read 'Creative Visualisation', written by Shakti Gawain. I learned in more detail how to use mental imagery to create what I wanted in my life. It involved not just positive thinking, but positive feeling. It's a bit like playing 'let's pretend' and then making it a reality.

I began to practise what I'd read, repeatedly visualising and imagining myself holding a baby of my own, feeling joyful as though it had already happened. Within less than a year, having been told that it was unlikely to ever happen, my much longed-for baby son miraculously came into the world and, almost three years later, I was further blessed to become the mother of a beautiful baby daughter.

● ●

Whatever the mind can conceive, it can achieve.
~ W. Clement Stone

The Power of Creative Visualisation

Creative visualisation is a powerful tool which can help you create the changes you want to make in your life. You may choose to create images of yourself in your mind's eye looking calm, relaxed, confident and happy, maybe fitter, healthier, more energised, maybe even a few pounds lighter. You can also use it to visualise yourself in the future having attracted whatever you want to have in your life: a loving relationship, a lovely home, a successful business or career, being financially secure, or on holiday in a place you've always wanted to visit...

"When you daydream you become unaware of your actual reality and your subconscious mind believes what you're experiencing in your virtual reality."

After creating the positive image in your mind's eye, it's important to not just see it but to also feel the associated emotions, as if you're already there. When you do this you're emitting out those powerful vibrations I talked about earlier and, like a magnet, attracting whatever it is that you want — as long as it's something positive and achievable! Each time you do this, as well as sending out positive vibrations, you are continuing to re-programme your subconscious mind, which is always recording whatever you're experiencing in your life. It will respond to your thoughts, beliefs and mental images by bringing what it's been programmed with into reality.

Just like a computer, if you install damaging programmes into your mind or allow it to be affected by viruses, it becomes corrupted and won't work in the way you want it to, but if you install positive, creative software into it, you'll be able to achieve great results. When you daydream you become unaware of your actual reality and your subconscious mind believes what you're experiencing in your virtual reality. This happens whether your daydreams are positive or negative, which is why it's so important to be aware of what you're thinking!

When you were a child, it's likely that you had a vivid imagination and could convince yourself that you were a particular character — perhaps becoming a super-hero or a princess, or playing 'mummies and daddies' and copying how you saw your parents acting. As we get older we grow out of doing this in a fun way but often start doing it in a negative way instead!

Have you ever worried about the possibility of something going wrong in the future then started to imagine how you'd feel if it did and, before you knew it, you were reacting as though it already had? Your imagination doesn't know the difference between a real and a strongly imagined experience, so if this can happen subconsciously in a negative way, you can use the same process consciously to imagine yourself having positive experiences.

When you repeatedly practise imagining yourself the way you want to be, rather than the way you don't want to be, you begin to reprogramme your subconscious mind to accept that the imagined you is the real you and it begins to do whatever it takes to make it happen.

"Successful athletes and performers have known for a long time that for peak performance it's just as important to use mental exercises to train their minds, as it is to physically exercise and train their bodies."

Successful athletes and performers have known for a long time that for peak performance it's just as important to use mental exercises to train their minds as it is to physically exercise and train their bodies. They visualise themselves achieving their personal best over and over again until they make it happen in reality. Over recent years, the power of creative visualisation has become more widely known about and a rapidly growing number of people from various walks of life are now using it to create success in all areas of their lives.

As well as being used for sports performance, it can be used in any number of situations where a person needs to perform an act or activity to the best of their ability. You could also use it to mentally rehearse giving a presentation or a speech, going for a job interview, or entering any situation where you feel out of your comfort zone, such as attending a gathering where you don't know anyone and would normally feel nervous.

The Anchor Technique exercise stems from an experiment carried out towards the late 1800's by a Nobel Prize winning scientist called Ivan Pavlov. You may have already heard of the 'Pavlov's Dogs Experiment'. During his experiment, Pavlov rang a bell each time he gave food to his dogs. After repeating this procedure a number of times, he rang the bell when the dogs were not eating or expecting to eat and the dogs began to salivate. The dogs had learned to associate the sound of the bell with their food and a new conditioned response had been learned.

Conditioned responses also happen naturally and can be triggered by any of the five senses. For example, you may hear a song on the radio which instantly triggers an emotion of sadness or happiness, which your subconscious mind has previously connected to the sound of the song, or you can smell a food or a fragrance which instantly takes you back to an associated memory from the past.

Phobias (irrational fears) are a good example of a conditioned response. When someone has an early frightening experience connected to a situation, place, creature or thing, their subconscious mind stores that information and, whenever they encounter a similar event in the future, even if there's no danger involved, the early memory is triggered causing the person to react fearfully.

During this exercise, while visualising and imagining yourself the way you want to look and feel, press together the forefinger and thumb of your dominant hand and hold them together until the positive feeling subsides. Each time you repeat the exercise your mind will build up an association between the two. Once this link has been made in your mind, you will be able to just press your fingers together and instantly get those positive feelings back — just like when Pavlov rang the bell and the dogs salivated.

Flying Lesson 9:
The Anchor Technique

This exercise combines using the Law of Attraction with a Neuro Linguistic Programming (NLP) exercise. NLP is a powerful therapy which helps you to change your mindset by using various exercises and techniques. As well as programming your subconscious mind to visualise and experience you as your ideal self, this technique gives you a tool to be able to bring those positive images and feelings back at any time you want to. Read right through the exercise before starting it...

When it's safe to do so, lie down or sit back comfortably, close your eyes and allow your body and your mind to relax. Next, imagine feeling the way you want to feel — calm, confident, happy, healthy, energised, organised, successful or anything else. Create an image of yourself in your mind's eye and notice, in as much detail as you can, your posture, your body language, your facial expression, the way you walk, talk, act and interact with others. To make the image more real, bring colour into it and make it life-size, then imagine going around to the back of the image and stepping into it, experiencing the situation first-hand.

Looking at the image from the outside is referred to as being *dissociated*; imagining yourself in the image is referred to as being *associated*. When you are associated with an image it feels far more real. Use the power of your mind to convince yourself for a few moments that you've made the changes you want to make and attracted into your life the things you want to happen and you really feel happy about it: a loving relationship, a lovely home, a new car, a successful business or career, being on holiday in a place you've always wanted to visit, or anything else.

Looking through the eyes of your ideal self, notice any sensations you're feeling or sounds you're hearing and talk to yourself in your head, perhaps saying things like *I feel so happy, I totally believe in myself, I can do it, I've done it, I feel great,* saying the words with enthusiasm while mentally punching the air!

You can imagine that the feelings you're experiencing have a colour and sense that colour flowing right through your body, out through your fingertips and down through the tips of your toes, infusing every fibre of your body. Make the colour brighter and more intense and feel it flowing out through your skin, over the surface of your body and surrounding you with a shield of calmness, confidence, success, love, happiness and anything else you want to feel.

While imagining you are already your ideal self in your ideal situation, you need to 'anchor' your feelings by pressing together the forefinger (pointing finger) and thumb of your dominant hand for as long as the feelings last. This may be anything between a few seconds and a few minutes; you may find they last longer as you continue to repeat the exercise. When the feelings begin to fade naturally, release your fingers and slowly open your eyes.

Repeat this process twice a day for several consecutive days, preferably when you've just woken up and just before you go to sleep. At these times of day you are in a drowsy state known as the 'theta' state, similar to the state of hypnosis, and your mind is more open to absorbing new images, messages and beliefs. If it's not possible for you to do it at these times, do it whenever works best for you.

Repetition of this exercise forms new neural pathways in your brain, creating a connection between your positive feelings and the simple physical action of pressing your forefinger and thumb together. Once this connection has been made, you'll be able to instantly bring back those feelings in any situation by simply pressing together your finger and thumb. There's nothing magical about the finger-thumb connection, but it's something you can do discreetly in public, without anyone else being aware of, to trigger the feelings you want to recreate.

Imagination is everything. It is the preview of life's forthcoming attractions.
— Albert Einstein

After being reminded about creative visualisation by watching 'The Secret', I started using it again and have since had lots of amazing personal experiences where my thoughts, feelings and vibrations have manifested 'miracles' into my life. Some have been big and some small but they've led me to intuitively know that this 'certain way of thinking' — and being — really does work for me.

Perhaps you had already discovered the LOA and have used it to manifest your own miracle, or maybe you're keen to start doing so. It could be that you've already tried using it and are frustrated because it didn't seem to work for you. If it's the latter, it could be that you have some subconscious fears or doubts about actually receiving the things you think you really want or that, deep down, you don't really believe it could possibly work for you.

If your subconscious thoughts and beliefs are not in line with your conscious desires, they will sabotage your ability to create those desires. If your negative inner-critic is still telling you that you don't really deserve what you desire, or those *yeah-buts* are adding themselves to the end of your desires (e.g. "I want to build a successful business...*yeah-but* it's probably not going to happen."), you'll be sending out contradictory messages into the universe and are likely to create your *yeah-buts* instead of your desires!

You might consciously tell yourself that you really want a promotion at work but deep down you're thinking that, although you'll be earning more money, the extra responsibility will be more stressful and you'll probably have to work late more often. Or you may feel you really want a romantic partner to share your life with but deep down you're reluctant to give up your freedom or you're afraid of being hurt.

You may be visualising and imagining what you want every day and using affirmations stating what you are now choosing to attract into your life but if you're feeling a desperate need for something, the message you're giving out to the universe is that you don't really believe you'll get it and that's what the universe hears and responds to. If you're worrying, feeling anxious or are jealous of the success you see other people having, you're likely to attract more things to feel worry about, feel anxious about and be jealous of.

Or, perhaps you're focusing on what you don't want. If you're thinking or saying to yourself, *I don't want to be poor/ be ill/ be alone* etc. the universe picks up on *be poor, be ill, be alone* as it doesn't process negatives. Remember what you learned in Step 2 about negatives? If I ask you not to think of a blue cow...what do you think of?

You can't avoid using the LOA, it's always working naturally whether or not you like it or even know about it. Remember what I told you earlier about the science behind the LOA — about those energy vibrations that are continuously being emitted by and attracted

"You are a powerful magnet continuously attracting what you focus your attention on..."

to the atoms in your cells? You are a powerful magnet continuously attracting what you focus your attention on...

You can choose to make the LOA work for you, rather than against you, by continuing to use the exercises, methods and techniques I've shared with you in this book. As Mike Dooley, author and speaker on 'The Secret' says, *Thoughts become Things.* You now have the tools to take control of your thoughts and can choose to focus only on the ones that will take you to your destination of Happiness!

The Hidden Messages in Water

In 1994, Japanese researcher and author of 'The Hidden Messages in Water', Dr. Masaru Emoto, carried out experiments which showed the different effects of positive and negative words on water. He froze distilled water in containers and then words or phrases were written on the containers or spoken to the frozen water, while different types of music were played within their environment.

The frozen water that was exposed to words like *I hate you, You are ugly, Anger* and to loud, unharmonious music, which most people would find uncomfortable to listen to, formed unattractive cloudy shapes within it. The frozen water that was exposed to phrases such as *I love you, You are beautiful, Peace* and to soothing relaxation or classical music formed beautiful crystals and patterns.

The photographs in his book clearly demonstrate the results of these experiments and are well worth viewing. When you consider that your body is around 65% water, just imagine how thinking negative thoughts is affecting you on a daily basis.

Dr. Emoto's experiments were featured in the film, 'What the Bleep do we know', which is part documentary and part story. It takes viewers on a journey to find answers to some questions — *What is our purpose? Where do we come from? What is reality?* — as we follow the journey of Amanda (Academy Award-winner Marlee Matlin), a divorcee who is less than happy with life, but who discovers a world where science meets spirituality, and her entire concept of reality is challenged.

Thoughts

Thoughts

Up above the clouds is a clear blue sky.

Collect Your Wings

Arrival at destination Happiness...

On arriving at your destination of Happiness, be aware that there may be times in the future when you're flying along smoothly and calmly then suddenly you hit turbulence. The up and down movement of a plane is a normal and natural part of flying and happens when the plane flies through air that's moving up and down. Turbulence is a normal occurrence for pilots and they're used to dealing with it on a regular basis, so you can just sit back with your seat belt fastened and trust that you're in safe hands.

It's also a normal and natural part of life to experience unexpected ups and downs, it's how you deal with them that matters. You could panic, become anxious, worry about what might happen, imagine the worst possible scenarios, or you can choose to stay calm, ride the storm, trust that you are safe and all will be well.

I've experienced a fair amount of turbulence along my journey but I've managed to rise above any storms and learned to fly higher. I had ups and downs during my counselling courses and then I soared when I discovered such great wisdom through the school of Practical Philosophy. I continued to fly higher, learning more and more through the many wonderful books I read and the training courses I attended in holistic health, reflexology, and nutrition.

I emerged from behind the clouds of my (dis)comfort zone and began sharing what I'd learned by facilitating courses, teaching others how to develop self-esteem, confidence and healthy relationships. I rose higher still and received further qualifications in Hypnosis, Clinical Hypnotherapy, Psychology, Psychotherapy, Neuro Linguistic Programming, Emotional Freedom Technique and Life Coaching.

Eventually, ten years after the all time low point of my life, when my plane had plunged to the ground leaving me feeling completely out of control, my wings were fully grown. I reached the stage where I felt empowered enough to open my own therapy practice and help clients take control of their lives as I'd learned to do.

Since that time my wings have spread even wider as I've continued to learn more about the mind, body and spirit as science and spirituality continue to merge through quantum physics. I am fascinated by new discoveries within neuroscience (the study of the brain and the nervous system and it's impact on behaviour) and epigenetics (which shows us that it's our mental, physical and emotional environment which affects our cells, not our genes). If you are interested in learning more about epignetics, I highly recommend Bruce

Lipton PhD's brilliant book, 'The Biology of Belief'.

All of this intriguing information continues to enlighten, energise and, at times, electrify me and I feel passionate about sharing it with anyone who is open to taking control of their lives, becoming self-empowered and creating their own happiness from within.

If you've completed your 7-step journey to emotional freedom, you'll have now learned how to:

1. Become aware of your subconscious programming and limiting beliefs.
2. Change your thoughts, feelings and beliefs with affirmations.
3. Take responsibility for your actions and reactions.
4. Control your mind through practising mindfulness.
5. Create a positive mental attitude.
6. Consistently feel a sense of appreciation and gratitude.
7. Use the power of universal energy and The Law of Attraction.

If you're just about to go back to Step 1 and embark on your journey, enjoy the lessons you learn along the way. By the time you arrive at your destination, you will have your wings and be feeling confident, positive, free, empowered, grateful, connected and happy. Have fun and remember that life is an on-going journey, so continue to use your tools and techniques, forever learning, growing and flying higher within the state of Happiness.

Dear Flyer,

I hope you enjoyed reading my book and that the tools and techniques contained in your flying lessons have helped you grow your wings! I'd really appreciate it if you could spare a few minutes to post a review on Amazon — or any other book website where it's being sold.

I'd love to know what you found particularly inspirational or useful. Your review doesn't have to take up much of your time, it can be brief and simple, perhaps just mentioning your favourite chapter and why you liked it.

You can also follow me and tweet me on Twitter to tell me what you thought — my username is @MsToniMackenzie — and if you wish, you can contact me by email at toni@innerdepths.co.uk

If you know anyone who you think would benefit from reading this book, please do tell them about it so that they can learn to fly too!

I'm looking forward to hearing from you!

Happy flying...

Toni

Flight Manuals

(Resources)

Several of the books listed below have been mentioned in the chapters of this book and all are recommended:

Bring out the Magic of your Mind ~ Al Koran
Creative Visualisation ~ Shakti Gawain
You Can Heal Your Life ~ Louise Hay
Feel the Fear and Do it Anyway ~ Susan Jeffers
Awareness ~ Anthony de Mello
The Road Less Travelled ~ M. Scott Peck
Love is Letting Go of Fear ~ Gerald G. Jampolsky
A Return to Love ~ Marianne Williamson
In The Meantime ~ Iyanla Vanzant
Emotional Intelligence ~ Daniel Goleman
The Alchemist ~ Paulo Coelho
The Prophet ~ Kahil Gibran
Real Magic ~ Wayne Dyer
Wishes Fulfilled ~ Wayne Dyer
The Power of Intention ~ Wayne Dyer
The Biology of Belief ~ Bruce Lipton
Spontaneous Evolution ~ Bruce Lipton
The Honeymoon Effect ~ Bruce Lipton
Power versus Force ~ David Hawkins
The Discovery ~ David Hawkins
You are the Placebo ~ Joe Dispenza
Breaking the Habit of Being Yourself ~ Joe Dispenza
Evolve Your Brain ~ Joe Dispenza
The Power of Now ~ Eckhart Tolle
A New Earth ~ Eckhart Tolle
Happiness ~ Matthieu Ricard

The Four Agreements ~ Don Miguel Ruiz
It's the Thought that Counts ~ David Hamilton
Why Kindness is Good for you ~ David Hamilton
I Heart Me ~ David Hamilton
Mindfulness ~ Mark Williams and Danny Penman
The Hidden Messages in Water ~ Masaru Emoto
The Secret ~ Rhonda Byrne
The Power ~ Rhonda Byrne
The Magic ~ Rhonda Byrne
The Science of Getting Rich ~ Walter Wattles
Infinite Possibilities ~ Mike Dooley
E-Squared ~ Pam Grout
E-Cubed ~ Pam Grout
Why Quantum Physicists Do Not Fail ~ Greg Kuhn
How Quantum Physicists Build New Beliefs ~ Greg Kuhn
Why Quantum Physicists Play Grow a Greater You ~ Greg Kuhn
Ask and it is Given ~ Esther & Jerry Hicks
The Amazing Power of Emotions ~ Esther & Jerry Hicks
The Vortex ~ Esther & Jerry Hicks

● ●

The following websites contain further useful information on the topics contained within this book:

www.innerdepths.co.uk
www.emofree.com
www.thetappingsolution.com
www.thesecret.tv
www.abraham-hicks.com
www.actionforhappiness.org

Author biography

Toni Mackenzie hung up her air stewardess hat many years ago, married a pilot and was happily cruising along when her plane unexpectedly descended into a crash landing. After many challenging life experiences and lessons, she gradually became stronger and wiser, eventually learning to fly again, this time higher than ever before...

As a self-empowerment coach, Toni now spends much of her time sharing the lessons that she has learned by speaking, writing and helping other people to create inner peace, freedom and happiness for themselves. The rest of the time she enjoys being mum to her grown-up son and daughter, and her two beautiful long-haired cats, as well as reading, practising yoga and qi-gong and dining out with friends in the many nearby restaurants of the Cheshire and Manchester area where she currently lives.